Highdays and Holidays

Jenny Bristow

GILL AND MACMILLAN
AND
ULSTER TELEVISION

Published in Ireland by
Gill and Macmillan Ltd
Goldenbridge
Dublin 8
with associated companies in
Auckland, Budapest, Gaborone, Harare, Hong Kong,
Kampala, Kuala Lumpur, Lagos, London, Madras
Manzini, Melbourne, Mexico City, Nairobi,
New York, Singapore, Sydney, Tokyo, Windhoek

Seventh impression 1992
Designed by Fergus O'Keeffe
Print origination by
Seton Music Graphics, Bantry, Co. Cork
Printed by Colour Books Ltd

Photographs by Kenneth McNally
Programme series produced and directed by
Ruth Johnston

British Library Cataloguing in Publication Data

Bristow, Jenny
Highdays and holidays.
I. Title 641.5

ISBN 0–7171–1923–8

This book is dedicated to my husband Bobby, whose wisdom echoes the words of Matthew Prior (1667–1726):
'Be to her virtues very kind.
Be to her faults a little blind.'

Contents

Preface

I was delighted and amazed by the overwhelming response to the television cookery programmes 'Kitchen Garden' and 'Highdays and Holidays' when they were transmitted by Ulster Television, and the need for a cookbook became evident. This book contains recipes from those two series and the latest, 'Highdays and Other Days'.

I am a devoted country lover, and when I married I exchanged one rural background for another one near Cullybackey, Co. Antrim. The essence of country life is scattered throughout the book: the use of elderflowers, honey and lavender ice cream served in a primose and violet ice bowl, blackberry mist, cranberries with quince or crab apples, and a pudding made using windfall pears, to name but a few. The recipes follow a healthier approach to cookery, and as far as possible the guidelines on reduced fat, sugar and salt and higher fibre content are followed.

While the trend in cooking and entertaining today is leaning more towards informality, there is always that special occasion to cook for; but whatever your cooking style make it fun, and remember that food is one of life's great pleasures.

I believe food should be a shared pleasure, a way of showing friendship, a way to celebrate a special occasion; and after all, can there be a better way of showing family and friends you care than by cooking for them?

My thanks to all the many enthusiastic people I met and worked with during the making of the programmes for Ulster Television and the writing of this book: to Lorraine and June Chesney, Anne Osbourne, Lorna Brownlee, Ann Morton, Helen Hamill, Masie Duncan and my family and many friends who so generously allowed me to borrow some of the items used in the programmes; to Martha Anderson, who typed the scripts for the book, Paula Wilson and Julie Millar for their invaluable help behind the scenes, and Dorothy Hayes, who put a shine on our lives as well as on the pots and pans; and to the Potato Marketing Board for the recipes for the potato fillings.

Adrienne Morgan and Patricia Moore, the production assistants, had the unenviable job, among others, of noting my every move; Rai Woods, the sound recordist, made sure that not a single word went unheard; Maurice Blair, the electrician, not only put light onto the food but also into our lives; and cameraman Sam Christie's filming techniques included bringing a gingerbread family to life.

Kenneth McNally, who took the photographs for the book, found locations around my home that I didn't even know existed. And finally to Ruth Johnston, who produced and directed the programmes.I have the greatest of admiration in her perfection as a programme maker. Her sense of humour and zest for life kept us all sane during the filming.

Conversion of Measurements

The following equivalents were used in converting between metric and imperial measurements:

Temperature

240 °C	475 °F	regulo 9
230 °C	450 °F	regulo 8
220 °C	425 °F	regulo 7
200 °C	400 °F	regulo 6
190 °C	375 °F	regulo 5
180 °C	350 °F	regulo 4
160 °C	325 °F	regulo 3
150 °C	300 °F	regulo 2
140 °C	275 °F	regulo 1
120 °C	250 °F	regulo ½
110 °C	225 °F	regulo ¼

Volume

3.4 L	6 pints
2.75 L	5 pints
2.25 L	4 pints
1.7 L	3 pints
1.4 L	2½ pints
1.1 L	2 pints
850 ml	1½ pints
570 ml	1 pint
425 ml	¾ pint
380 ml	⅔ pint
280 ml	½ pint
200 ml	7 fl. oz
170 ml	6 fl. oz
140 ml	¼ pint/5 fl. oz
115 ml	4 fl. oz
70 ml	⅛ pint

Weight

1.35 kg	3 lb
900 g	2 lb
680 g	1½ lb
450 g	1 lb
400 g	14 oz
340 g	12 oz
285 g	10 oz
225 g	8 oz
200 g	7 oz
170 g	6 oz
140 g	5 oz
115 g	4 oz
85 g	3 oz
70 g	2½ oz
55 g	2 oz
45 g	1½ oz
30 g	1 oz
15 g	½ oz

1. In Celebration of . . .

A buffet is by far the best and easiest way to entertain a large number of people. There are many advantages in giving a buffet, but for me it is the fact that planning and preparation and cooking can be spread over a number of days, leaving you free to enjoy the last-minute preparations. There are many occasions when a buffet-style meal is suitable: christenings, silver weddings, luncheon parties, children's birthday parties. But for me the best has to be the one provided by my mum single-handed for our wedding day. I well remember the evening before the big event. those late relations arriving with presents, being speedily relieved of their gift and set to work preparing the bowls of strawberries.

When cooking for special occasions such as buffets it is a good idea to have a theme: colour, style, china to be used, flowers, or wine. The initial planning is most important to the finished table: so often buffets are a chance to celebrate events that happen once in a lifetime.

I have chosen an unusual combination of foods, which I feel should suit all tastes. The celebration chicken is a cold chicken dish that has a very tasty, lightly curried sauce: a crunchy dish that is served cold with an assortment of lettuce leaves. This dish gives variety, especially to those who are watching the calories.

The creamy lasagne can be prepared and frozen well ahead of time. This is excellent party food: economical, attractive, and easily served. This dish is very popular, and the texture can be varied by the use of wholewheat lasagne or lasagne verdi.

A cold salmon makes a striking centrepiece to any table, and I find my freezer is always well stocked, as my mother, sister and brother are enthusiastic and successful fisherfolk, even smoking the salmon in the home smokery!

Salmon needs a good sauce, and the seafood sauce made by the blender method is much easier and holds extremely well. Cucumber, prawns, avocados, mussels—all will liven it up, depending on the budget.

Salads that can be made ahead of time are very useful. A cold potato salad is very versatile with all flavours, and keeps well, especially if you toss the potatoes in a little lemon juice before cooking. The colour is much whiter and it prevents the blackening that often occurs with the later season's potatoes.

The hazelnut and grape meringue and port wine jelly look attractive when served on the buffet table. Do remember that buffet food must be very easy to eat. It can be difficult to balance plates, glasses, forks and spoons all at once, so consider the choice of food carefully.

Canapés or finger food are always a good way to get the party started. Keep them small, and provide a variety: cherry tomatoes with cream cheese, asparagus and brown bread rolls, prawn and cucumber crackers, dill and smoked salmon rolls, cheese kebabs, stilton and celery boats—all look attractive if served together on a large tray.

Cucumber Mousse

It should serve 6–8 people if used on the buffet table; if used as a starter I feel the quantities would stretch to 10.

450 g (1 lb) spiced and diced cucumber (marinated in vinegar)
55 g (2 oz) low-fat yoghurt
55 g (2 oz) mayonnaise
55 g (2 oz) cream cheese or quark
} **or a combination of these three ingredients**
Assorted herbs
Whipped cream (6 dessertsp.)
15 g (½ oz) gelatine dissolved in 6 dessertsp. stock or water
1 egg white

Marinate the finely chopped cucumber in a bowl with cider vinegar or a flavoured vinegar of your choice. Heat the gelatine gently over a low heat and add the liquid or stock to it. Remove from the heat when the gelatine has become opaque. Add to the already mixed mayonnaise, yoghurt, and cheese, mixing well. Add the herbs, chopped cucumber, egg white, and cream, and fold gently until well mixed.

Serve in individual goblets or glasses, or pour into an angel cake mould with a centre hole. Refrigerate for 1 hour until firm, then unmould. I like to serve this quantity with a matchstick salad of celery, nuts, and apple.

Serves 6–8

Ma King's Salmon

Allow 125–175 g (4–6 oz) per person. When calculating the amount you need, remember that the head, fins and tail account for one-fifth of the total weight of a fish.

1 salmon, 2–2.5 kg (4–5 lb)
Salt and freshly milled pepper
3.5 L (6 pints) cold water
2–3 tablesp. white wine
1 carrot, sliced
2 bay leaves
A few stalks of parsley
½ lemon, cut into slices
4–5 black peppercorns
½ onion, sliced

Clean and gut the salmon, taking care to remove the insides and the dark membrane that runs down the backbone. (Do not remove the head or scales at this stage.) Brush the surface of the fish well with oil to protect it during cooking. Place on the trivet of a fish kettle, and add all other ingredients, checking that the water just covers the fish. Bring to the boil on the lowest heat possible, and turn off the heat immediately boiling point is reached.

Leave the fish sitting, preferably overnight, then lift it out, descale it, and serve.

Serves 14–16

Seafood Sauce

This seafood sauce is similar to blender hollandaise sauce.

4 egg yolks
1 teasp. caster sugar
1 tablesp. tarragon vinegar
1 tablesp. lemon juice
225 g (8 oz) melted butter
2–3 dessertsp. whipped cream
A few pink peppercorns
115–170 g (4–6 oz) peeled prawns
A few drops of Tabasco sauce

Whisk the eggs and sugar over a pan of warm water for 2–3 minutes until slightly creamy. Transfer to a blender or food processer and whisk for 30 seconds. Slowly trickle in the vinegar and lemon juice while they are both warm, whisking continually. Finally add the melted butter—as slowly as possible, otherwise the sauce will end up too thin.

Transfer to a bowl, then add the whipped cream, peeled prawns, peppercorns, and a few drops of Tabasco sauce.

Serves 10–12

Hot Spicy Lasagne

Bolognese Sauce

450 g (1 lb) minced steak
1 onion
115 g (4 oz) streaky bacon
2 cloves of garlic
½ red pepper
½ green pepper
1 chilli
½ teasp. chilli powder
½ teasp. oregano
1 dessertsp. cooking oil
1 large can of tomatoes

Pasta

225 g (8 oz) lasagne
1 dessertsp. olive oil
Boiling water

Cream Sauce

55 g (2 oz) butter
55 g (2 oz) flour
570 ml (1 pint) milk
Pinch of nutmeg
2 tablesp. whipping cream
115 g (4 oz) grated parmesan cheese

Start by making the bolognese sauce. Fry the onion in a large pan in the hot oil, with the garlic. Add the finely chopped peppers, chilli, bacon, seasoning, and minced steak. Cook all the ingredients well together for 4–5 minutes, then add the tinned tomatoes and simmer for 15–20 minutes.

To cook the lasagne the secret lies in adding the sheets to the boiling water and boil one sheet at a time. Cook for 6–7 minutes, then lift out the sheets individually and place them in a bowl of cold water. Leave to stand—they won't come to any harm.

The white sauce is made by the roux method. Melt the fat in a saucepan, add the flour, mix well, and then add the milk, stirring as the milk reaches boiling point. Cook for at least 30 seconds, remove from the heat, and add the nutmeg and whipped cream. Finally layer the three stages in a lasagne dish, being careful not to overlap the pasta; and alternate the layers: meat, pasta, sauce. Repeat the layering, and sprinkle the top layer with grated parmesan cheese. Bake in the oven at 160 °C (325 °F or regulo 3) for 25–50 minutes.

Serves 8–10

Celebration Chicken

This is one of my favourite cold chicken dishes. It is ideal for a buffet, and can be made up to 12 hours in advance.

450g (1 lb) chicken pieces
1 dessertsp. cooking oil
1 tablesp. honey
A few drops of soy sauce
225 g (8 oz) green grapes
225 g (8 oz) black grapes
225 g (8 oz) fresh or tinned pineapple
2 stalks of celery

Sauce

1 dessertsp. oil
Bunch of spring onions
2 dessertsp. apricot jam
2 dessertsp. lemon juice
2 teasp. curry paste
280 ml (½ pint) mayonnaise
Squeeze of tomato purée

To make the sauce, lightly fry the spring onions in a little hot oil, and coat well. To this add the lemon juice, sieved apricot jam, and curry paste. When slightly cooled add the mayonnaise and mix well. Tomato purée can also be added; this very much improves the colour of the sauce.

Lightly pan-fry the chicken pieces with the honey and soy sauce: this greatly improves the flavour of the chicken. Make sure the chicken is well cooked—approximately 10–15 minutes—then add all the juices with the chicken to the sauce. Add the grapes, pineapple and celery to the chicken and sauce, mixing well.

Serve cold on a bed of seasonal lettuce.

Serves 6–8

Port Wine Jelly

850 ml (1½ pints) water
225 g (8 oz) caster sugar
140 ml (¼ pint) port
280 ml (½ pint) lemon juice
55 g (2 oz) gelatine
170 ml (6 fl. oz) water (to dissolve)

Crimson Fruit Salad

115 g (4 oz) cranberries
115 g (4 oz) blackberries
1 tablesp. water
30 g (1 oz) demerara sugar
55 g (2 oz) strawberries
2 plums
1 tablesp. lemon and orange juice
A few red cherries

Into a large pan place the water, lemon juice, sugar, and port, stirring well until the sugar dissolves. Add the dissolved gelatine, being careful not to overheat it or it will 'kill' the action of the gelatine. Pour into a 1 L (2 pint) mould and leave in the fridge to set, preferably overnight; then unmould.

For the fruit salad gently poach the cranberries and blackberries in a pan with the water and sugar until they just start to soften. Add the sliced plums, strawberries, cherries, and any other soft seasonal fruits.

Toss in a little orange and lemon juice and serve around the jelly.

Serves 10–12

Hazelnut and Grape Meringue

4 egg whites
225 g (8 oz) caster sugar
115 g (4 oz) chopped hazelnuts
3 circles of greaseproof paper 175 mm (7 in.) in diameter

Praline Filling

115 g (4 oz) hazelnuts
3 teasp. water
55 g (2 oz) caster sugar
140 ml (¼ pint) whipped cream

Chocolate Filling

170 g (6 oz) melted chocolate
1 dessertsp. coffee essence
A little Grand Marnier
140 ml (¼ pint) whipped cream

To make the meringue, whisk the egg white with half the sugar until it is stiff but not dry. Carefully fold in the remainder of the sugar and the chopped hazelnuts. Divide the mixture onto the three circles of waxed paper, spreading it out until it comes just to the edge of the circle. Bake at 140 °C (275 °F or regulo 1) for 1 to 1½ hours.

Praline Filling

Dissolve the sugar in the water over gentle heat. Bring to the boil and boil for 4 minutes or until the syrup is a light golden-brown colour. Stir in the hazelnuts, then pour onto a lightly oiled baking tray lined with non-stick silicone or waxed paper. When the praline is cold, crush it with a rolling pin or in a blender, then leave it aside.

Melt the chocolate over a gentle heat, stir in the instant coffee and Grand Marnier, cool slightly, then add to the whipped cream. Alternately layer the sheets of meringue with the fillings, sandwich together, and decorate with little bunches of grapes.

2. What's to Eat, Mum?

I give three birthday parties every year, and I enjoy them every bit as much as the children do. One thing I have found is that children expect plenty of variety: a different birthday cake for every occasion, and an imagination that's unending.

There are still the firm family favourites that appear year after year, such as the gingerbread family, and aren't they fun to decorate! With my three children, bags of icing, and an assortment of colourful decorations, the sky is the limit—and so is the clearing up!

Tommy the tortoise birthday cake has a healthy sponge made with grated carrot and sunflower oil. Food for children should be plentiful and very simple; I find they don't like rich, highly seasoned food. Give them wholesome food they know, and add your own usual touches. I have learnt from bitter experience to scale the portions down in size, and to make sure they are all the same size! Children like to eat a little of everything; and after all, if they have been brought up to enjoy a good healthy diet, then on highdays and holidays, treats are in order.

I find fondant icing good for birthday cakes, made with liquid glucose, which is very pliable to work with and is usually available.

Making triple-decker sandwiches is a good way of encouraging children to eat wholemeal bread, with a layer disguised in the middle and assorted fillings. There is such a variety of cutters and shapes to make sandwiches look good; or why not turn them into pin-wheels or funny faces!

Don't feel a bit guilty if you resort to ready-made convenience food for parties or simply for tea. I have included some of my stand-by family favourites for busy children always on the go: the prehistoric sausage rolls made with puff pastry, the crispy fish rolls garnished with potato crisps, and the quick mini-pizzas.

Mothers appear to get busier every year and the demands on them greater, so with these ideas in mind I have put together some recipes that I hope will take some of the stress out of cooking.

On a more serious note, do remember that in cooking for our children we are laying down the foundation of their eating habits for the rest of their lives.

Mariner's Crispy Bake

This is one of the best recipes I have for encouraging children to eat fish. Used here with a crispy topping of potato crisps and cheese, it is always popular.

6 fillets of plaice or lemon sole
6 rashers of back or streaky bacon
30 g (1 oz) polyunsaturated fat
Rind of ½ lemon and juice
1 packet of potato crisps
55 g (2 oz) cheddar cheese
30 g (1 oz) wholemeal breadcrumbs

Skin the fillets of plaice and sprinkle with lemon rind and juice. Place the rasher on a board, put the fish on top of the bacon, and roll it up with the fish on the inside. Arrange the fish rolls in an ovenproof dish, sprinkle the topping of cheese, crisps and crumbs over the top, and bake in the oven at 200 °C (400 °F or regulo 6) for 15–20 minutes. (Note that cooking time will vary according to the size of the fish fillets.)

Serves 6

Bert's Prehistoric Sausage Roll

My tin contains an assortment of prehistoric animal cutters, which younger children adore, and they are always willing to help to cut out the pastry shapes.

450 g (1 lb) ready-made puff or flaky pastry
450 g (1 lb) sausage meat
55 g (2 oz) breadcrumbs
1 large onion, grated
1 tablesp. chopped parsley
½ teasp. mustard
1 beaten egg

Mix all the filling ingredients together with ½ egg in a bowl, then roll out, shaping into a log. Roll out the pastry into a rectangle approximately 250 by 200 mm (10 by 8 in.). Run a pastry lattice cutter along half of the pastry. Place the sausage log on the centre of the other half of the pastry, brush the edges with beaten egg, and seal well together. Flute the edges, then brush the top well with milk or egg and garnish the top with shapes cut from pastry. Bake in the oven at 240 °C (475 °F or regulo 9) for 10 minutes and then reduce heat to 190 °C (375 °F or regulo 5) for 20–25 minutes.

Mini-Pizza

115 g (4 oz) self-raising flour
115 g (4 oz) wholemeal flour
¼ teasp. salt
1 teasp. baking powder
55 g (2 oz) margarine
1 egg
A little milk to mix to a soft dough

Topping

2 tomatoes
115 g (4 oz) grilled finely chopped bacon or sardines
4 tablesp. tomato ketchup
55 g (2 oz) grated cheddar cheese
Chopped parsley to garnish

Make the pizza base by mixing the sieved flours with the salt and baking powder. Cut and rub in the margarine. Add the lightly beaten egg and sufficient milk to mix to a soft dough. Knead lightly on a floured surface, then roll out approximately 25 mm (1 in.) thick and 50–70 mm (2–3 in.) in diameter. Blend together the tomato ketchup, grated cheese, and chopped bacon. Brush the pizzas with a little oil, then spread the topping on the sliced tomatoes. Bake in a pre-heated oven at 200 °C (400 °F or regulo 6) for 10–12 minutes.

Garnish with a little parsley; serve cold or warm, but not too hot.

Kiddies' Banger and Mash Lasagne

1 large onion
1 dessertsp. oil
225 g (8 oz) low-fat pork sausages
225 g (8 oz) baked beans
225 g (8 oz) grated cheese or cottage cheese
225 g (8 oz) no-cook lasagne
2–3 lightly boiled sliced potatoes
115 g (4 oz) garden peas
1 carton low-fat yoghurt
1 egg

Lightly fry the onion until soft and lightly brown, then mix with the baked beans. Lightly grill the sausages, then slice at an angle; leave to cool slightly. Arrange the lasagne: beans, sausages, peas and potatoes in an ovenproof rectangular dish with layers of pasta. Prepare the topping by mixing the yoghurt, lightly beaten egg and cheese together, and cover the lasagne. Bake in the oven at 220 °C (425 °F or regulo 7) for 25–30 minutes. Reduce the temperature after 10 minutes to allow the lasagne to cook slowly.

Serves 4

The Gingerbread Family

To make 4–6 gingerbread men.

225 g (8 oz) plain flour
1 teasp. baking soda
1½ teasp. ginger powder
55 g (2 oz) soft brown sugar
85 g (3 oz) fat
1 egg, lightly beaten
Assorted decorations: ribbons, sweets, icing

Mix all the dry ingredients together in a bowl: flour, baking soda, ginger powder, and soft brown sugar. Add the fat to the dry ingredients, and mix. Finally add the beaten egg, mixing well, then turn the mixture out onto a floured board and knead well. Make the mixture about 10 mm (⅜ in.) in thickness. Bake at 180 °C (350 °F or regulo 4) for 15 minutes, and decorate when cool.

Peter's Very Hungry Caterpillar

The children will adore helping to make this one. Don't worry if it turns out differently each time! Serves 4–6, depending on the number and size of the swiss rolls.

4–6 miniature chocolate swiss rolls
1 packet Smarties
A few chocolate matchsticks and a small chocolate truffle
115 g (4 oz) coconut, coloured

Cut the chocolate swiss rolls in half, then place them on a plate in caterpillar fashion. Use the truffle for its head, smarties for the eyes, chocolate matchsticks for antennas. Serve on a plate or cake board that you have sprinkled with green coconut (this is simply coconut to which a few drops of green food colouring have been added).

Rachel Jane's Fairy Cakes

55 g (2 oz) butter or margarine
55 g (2 oz) caster sugar
1 egg
70 g (2½ oz) flour
¼ teasp. baking powder
Rind of ½ lemon
A little milk if necessary
115 g (4 oz) currants (optional)

Cream the butter and sugar thoroughly. Beat in the lightly whisked egg gradually. With the last of the egg, add the flour and a little milk if necessary. Finally add the lemon rind and fruit. Two-thirds fill greased patty tins and bake in a fairly hot oven for 15 minutes: approximately 200 °C (400 °F or regulo 6).

Makes 10–12

Chocolate Mice

12 fairy cakes
115 g (4 oz) melted chocolate
12 marshmallows
24 chocolate buttons
2 dessertsp. butter cream icing
Liquorice and sweets to decorate

Slice the top of the fairy cakes and cover with melted chocolate on top. Place a marshmallow on top of each one, then spoon or cover the marshmallow with chocolate. Put the chocolate buttons in place for the ears, and use the butter cream to make eyes and a mouth. Use liquorice for the whiskers and currants for the eyes.

Tommy the Tortoise Birthday Cake

This is a very healthy birthday cake for children, the filling being high in fibre and low in fat. It has a very distinctive texture and lovely colour.

140 ml (¼ pint) sunflower oil
115 g (4 oz) caster sugar
2 eggs lightly beaten
115 g (4 oz) self-raising flour
115 g (4 oz) grated carrot
2 dessertsp. apricot jam to brush

Into a bowl add the sunflower oil and caster sugar, mixing well (but the sugar will not dissolve at this stage). Whisk the eggs lightly and add alternately with the flour, mixing well until the consistency is smooth. Next add the coarsely grated carrot, and when evenly mixed transfer to a lightly greased 570 ml (1 pint) pudding basin. Cook either in the microwave for 4–5 minutes or the oven at 180 °C (350 °F or regulo 4) for 20–25 minutes or until firm to touch.

Fondant Icing

450 g (1 lb) icing sugar
1 dessertsp. liquid glucose
1 egg white

Place all the ingredients into a bowl and mix well together in the food processor; this should take no longer than 1 minute. Should the icing become hard, sprinkle it with a little cold water. Store it in a polythene bag until ready for use. Cut off one-third of the icing and reserve it for the decorations.

To Decorate the Cake

Cover the cake when cool with a little apricot jam so that the fondant icing will stick, then cover it with the rolled-out icing. (Note that a portion of the cake has been cut away to allow for the neck of the tortoise.) Smooth the icing with your hands, which have been dusted with a little icing sugar. Using the garrett frill cutter, finish the bottom edge of the cake with a frill; attach the frill, sticking with a little egg white. Colour the remaining third of the icing with two colours. Roll out, place one piece on top of the other, roll up, allow to firm a little, then cut thin slices from the roll and flatten slightly—this creates the shell pattern for the top.

Decorate the cake using toffees for the head and feet, sweets for the eyes and mouth, and the coloured icing to create the shell pattern. Serve on a plate or cake board sprinkled with green coconut.

Serves 10–14

Kiddy Kebabs

These kebabs go down really well at children's parties. Cocktail sticks are fine for the older children, provided they are being supervised and the cocktail sticks are collected afterwards.

Wedges of—
- **Strawberries**
- **Oranges**
- **Grapes**
- **Cheese**
- **Ham or sardines**
- **Kiwi fruit**
- **Apples**

Cut small wedges of the fruits, cheese, and ham, put them on cocktail sticks and place into a potato or orange covered with tinfoil.

3. A Family Affair

Sunday is a day for the family, and after all, isn't it the day when you can make the family feel just that little bit more special, and what better way than cooking for them! Sunday lunch is usually a traditional meal in our house, with a good warming soup, rarely a starter, a main course that looks after itself in the oven, plenty of lightly cooked assorted vegetables, roast potatoes, and a real pudding to finish off.

Even the cook needs a day off, and I feel Sunday meals should be planned with that aim in mind. Use the longer, slower methods of cooking, such as roasting, which changes the pace of the day. It's a day to forget about precision timing, to eat when the food is cooked.

The secret of success in Sunday cooking is that as much as possible should be prepared in advance, leaving the morning free; and here I have put together a meal that after the initial preparation can be cooked entirely in the oven.

The vicarage soup is a real flavoursome warming soup with a light chicken stock. I believe good stock is the essence of any good soup. Stock can be made in bulk and kept in the freezer and used on demand. I vary this soup depending on the seasonal availability of vegetables; I prefer garden peas in June and artichokes in December.

My daily bread is named for its simplicity and the fact that it is made practically every day in our home.

The applejack pork, using pork steaks with a very tasty stuffing, is cooked in cider to give a very different flavour. Don't worry about using cider for the family, as the alcohol content will evaporate during the initial cooking. This can either be cooked on the hob or done in the oven along with the vegetables.

Lightly steamed assorted vegetables can be livened up with just a little imagination: honey on the parsnips, thatch made of onion, cheese and wholemeal breadcrumbs sprinkled over the cabbage and baked in the oven for 5–10 minutes, and sesame seeds dusted on the roast potatoes.

Sunday is a day for puddings rather than desserts, and cobblers are among the simplest puddings, being little more than fruit with a crust. Any sort of fruit can be used: apricots, quince, berries, plums, peaches, or, in wintertime, when fruits are not so plentiful, dried fruits combined with the reliable cooking apple. My favourites are blackberry or gooseberry dusted with brown sugar and elderflower heads; I find elderflowers have great affinity with gooseberries. My foolish sauce is based on the fruit fool dessert and has endless varieties, again depending on the fruits in season.

Elderflower wine is a bubbly, refreshing drink made from the pretty elderflower heads that bloom so profusely in May and June. Use corks for the lemonade, and don't worry if the occasional one pops: put it in again—but drink it soon!

Vicarage Soup

1 potato, finely chopped
2 carrots
A few small leeks, chopped into rings
1 tablesp. oil
1.1 L (2 pints) chicken stock
225 g (8 oz) chicken pieces, cooked
Salt and pepper
2–3 dessertsp. fresh parsley

Fry the diced potato and sliced carrot together in a little hot oil, tossing well to make sure that the vegetables are evenly coated. Chop or slice the leeks into fine rings, add to the pan, and continue cooking for a further 2–3 minutes. Season well. Remove the flesh from the chicken bones that have been used to make the stock, and add to the soup along with the strained chicken stock. Add a generous sprinkling of fresh garden parsley, place the lid on top, and simmer gently for a further 15–20 minutes.

Serve hot with granary bread.

Serves 6

My Daily Bread

Cracked wheat is simply the crushed grains of wheat. If I find it difficult to obtain I use pinhead oatmeal instead.

225 g (8 oz) self-raising flour
55 g (2 oz) wholemeal flour
30 g (1 oz) cracked wheat
Pinch of salt
30 g (1 oz) fat
1 egg
140 ml (¼ pint) approx. buttermilk

Sieve the self-raising flour into a bowl; add a pinch of salt, wholemeal flour, and half the cracked wheat. Mix together, then add the fat, first chopping through then rubbing in until evenly mixed. Make a well in the centre of the flour, then add the beaten egg and buttermilk to mix to a soft but not sticky dough. Knead lightly, turn onto a floured board, make into a round shape like a cob, and place on a floured baking sheet. Make a cross on top, brush with beaten egg, and sprinkle with the remaining half of the cracked wheat. Bake for 20–25 minutes at 220 °C (425 °F or regulo 7).

Serves 6

Applejack Pork

6–8 pork steaks, each approximately 100g (4 oz)

Stuffing

170 g (6 oz) white breadcrumbs
1 onion, chopped
1 cooking apple
30 g (1 oz) fat
1 egg
A little parsley
Black pepper
280 ml (½ pint) cider
400 g (14 oz) tinned tomatoes
A few cloves

Place the pork steaks between sheets of greaseproof paper and beat with a rolling-pin to flatten them.

To make the stuffing, add to the breadcrumbs the chopped apple, onion, fat, and parsley, using the egg to bind the stuffing together. Divide the stuffing between the pork rolls, packing down well; roll up, and tie with string to secure. Fry in a little hot oil to brown and seal in the juices, making sure it is evenly browned on all sides. Add the cider, tinned tomatoes, and cloves. The cooking time improves the flavour, and the alcohol content evaporates. Put the lid on, and place in the oven to cook for approximately 1 hour at 190 °C (375 °F or regulo 5).

Garnish with chervil and wedges of apple. Season to taste.

Serves 6–8

Honeyed Parsnips

Cut the parsnips into four lengthwise. Steam for 2–3 minutes, then place in a roasting tin. Pour over 1 tablesp. of oil and a little honey (approximately 2 tablesp.). Bake for 20–25 minutes or until tender at 180 °C (350 °F or regulo 4).

Parsnips in Hiding

When the older parsnips require a slightly longer cooking time, this is a most unusual way of preparing them, by combining them with a batter.

4–6 parsnips
30 g (1 oz) fat
1 dessertsp. honey
Salt and pepper
140 g (5 oz) plain flour
2 eggs
280 ml (½ pint) milk (or a mixture of water and milk)
A pinch of mustard

Peel the parsnips well and discard the woody areas, then blanch for just 1–2 minutes. Toss the chunks of parsnips in a pan with the melted fat, honey, and seasoning. Turn frequently, coating on all sides. Grease 10–12 patty tins, then make the batter. Sieve flour, seasoning and mustard powder into a bowl. Make a well in the centre and add the eggs and milk, beating thoroughly to make a smooth batter. Divide the parsnips in honey into the tins, pour on the batter, and bake for 15–20 minutes at 220 °C (425 °F or regulo 7).

Cabbage Under Thatch

A rather different way of serving boiled or lightly steamed cabbage. Place it in a serving dish and sprinkle over the top 55 g (2 oz) of breadcrumbs mixed with 55 g (2 oz) of grated cheese and 1 dessertsp. of finely chopped onion. Bake at 180 °C (350 °F or regulo 4) for 5–10 minutes, or brown under the grill.

Farmhouse Casserole with Potato and Herb Cobbler

This dish is very easy to prepare, and can be cooked in the oven or on the hob. The addition of the potato and herb cobbler turns it into a complete meal on its own.

450 g (1 lb) braising or stewing steak
170 g (6 oz) ox kidney (optional)
½ turnip
2 parsnips } **cut into matchsticks**
2 carrots
kohlrabi (hamburg parsley could also be used)
2–3 diced potatoes
115 g (4 oz) split peas
1 bay leaf
1 large onion
570 ml (1 pint) approx. stock or water
Seasoning

Cobbler

225 g (8 oz) self-raising flour
Pinch of salt
1 teasp. chopped parsley, tarragon, or rosemary
55 g (2 oz) potatoes, cooked and sieved
55 g (2 oz) unsaturated margarine
4 dessertsp. approx. milk
1 egg to glaze
Garnish of chopped parsley

Cut the steak into cubes and toss it with the onion into hot oil. Place the lid on top and fry gently for 15–20 minutes. Add the vegetables, evenly cut into matchstick strips. Mix the split peas, bay leaf, seasoning, and stock. Reduce the heat and simmer gently for approximately 45 minutes or until tender. If the vegetables are tossed in lemon juice it will improve the colour during cooking.

Prepare the cobbler by sieving all the dry ingredients together. Rub in the potatoes and margarine; add the herbs; add milk to form a soft dough. Roll out the scone topping until it is 12 mm (½ in.) thick and, using a 50 mm (2 in.) cutter, cut out approximately 12 scones. Arrange the scones on top of the steak and vegetables, overlapping around the edge. Glaze with beaten egg and cook at 200 °C (400 °F or regulo 6) for 20–25 minutes or until golden-brown in colour.

Serve garnished with parsley. (Cooking time is the same whether using hob or oven.)

Serves 6–8

Gooseberry Cobbler

225 g (8 oz) gooseberries
30 g (1 oz) demerara sugar
A few elderflower heads

Rich Shortcrust Pastry

285 g (10 oz) self-raising flour
140 g (5 oz) fat
30 g (1 oz) caster sugar
140 ml (¼ pint) milk

Top and tail the gooseberries, place them in a bowl, and sprinkle them with sugar and finely chopped elderflower heads. Leave this to sit for at least 15–30 minutes, when the gooseberries will take on a lovely flavour.

To make the pastry, sieve the flour into a bowl, add the fat, rubbing it in until fine, and add the sugar and sufficient milk to mix to a soft but firm dough. Roll out the pastry and divide it into six even-sized squares, brush the edges with cold water, and spoon on the gooseberries and elderflower, dividing them evenly among the six squares. Fold up the edges, place in an ovenproof dish, and bake at 160 °C (325 °F or regulo 3) for 20–25 minutes. Serve with the sauce.

My Foolish Sauce

The secret of this recipe is to keep the temperature low and not to overcook the custard.

280 ml (½ pint) milk
2 egg yolks
15 g (½ oz) cornflour, blended
115 ml (4 fl. oz) puréed gooseberries

Warm the milk but do not boil, and to this add the lightly beaten egg, to which the cornflour has been added. Stir well until it shows signs of thickening. Add the puréed gooseberries, mix well, and serve the sauce either hot or cold. Sweeten to taste.

Elderflower Wine

Elderflowers bloom in May and June.

2.25 L (4 pints) lukewarm water
340 g (12 oz) caster or granulated sugar
Juice and coarse peel of 1 lemon
7–8 heads of elderflower
1 dessertsp. cider vinegar

Dissolve the sugar in the lukewarm water, either in a bowl or over gentle heat. To this add the lemon juice, rind, cider vinegar, and well-washed elderflower heads, submerging them in the liquid. Leave aside for 24 hours in a covered bowl, then strain the wine through muslin into sterilised bottles (corks are better than screw tops). Set aside for two weeks, and during this time the wine will become fizzy.

Serve chilled with ice and lemon.

4. After Eight

Giving a dinner party is one of those occasions most of us have to cope with at some time or another, and it can either be a lot of fun or a real nightmare. However, you can turn it into an occasion that, with careful planning and preparation, can be enjoyable for everyone.

The dinner party is a chance to impress your guests, and a small dinner party is one of the best ways to enjoy good food and good conversation. The choice of menu is most important to allow time to spend at the table instead of at the sink.

Ideally, plan at least one cold course, or, if it is a summer party, you can easily get away with more. In this menu I have chosen a cold starter (the stilton and pear mousse), one cold pudding (the wild strawberry cake), and Rosie's rhubarb, which can be served either warm or cold.

The stilton and pear mousse can be made up to three days in advance and stored in the fridge, and half an hour before serving unmoulded and garnished. If possible leave the first course on the table.

It is not always necessary to serve soup with a starter, but on the more formal occasion a light soup such as lettuce with mint is colourful, tangy, and easily prepared.

Making the decisions on the main course can often be the most difficult part. Keep it light; so often we tend to go overboard with our generosity and leave guests feeling too full. Casseroles are excellent, as is the economical salmon under wraps. In this dish the filling is limited only by your imagination: pork, lamb or chicken can be used as an alternative to salmon.

A tossed green salad makes a light accompaniment to little new potatoes with yoghurt and lemon dressing. There is an enormous variety of greens today, including watercress, lamb's lettuce, and curly endive; and deep-red radishes tossed in a honey dressing create a most attractive dish.

Pasta is becoming increasingly popular, especially among the young, and offers endless variety.

A contrast of puddings is a good idea if two are to be served, and these have the advantage of not usually requiring last-minute attention. Ice cream is always popular: try the honey and lavender ice cream (page 92), or just a good vanilla with a hot sauce.

The extras are I feel what add to a dinner party. It is a matter of choice whether the cheese is served before or after the pudding; I like to serve it before as an alternative for those people who prefer to miss the pudding.

Make sure the cheese is removed from the fridge at least an hour before serving, to allow the flavours to develop. I prefer quality rather than quantity, and serve no more than four. Don't forget about the goat's cheese now widely available.

Home-made sweets are well worth the effort and look so well when served at coffee time. More and more people are turning to decaffeinated coffee, so do offer a choice to round off the meal. And enjoy yourself; after all, the aim of the evening is to be with the people you have invited.

Stilton and Pear Mousse

115 g (4 oz) Stilton cheese
140 ml (¼ pint) low-fat yoghurt
2 comice pears } **to pickle**
1 teasp. lemon juice }
1 tablesp. cider vinegar }
1 egg white
15 g (½ oz) gelatine
1 tablesp. water

Finely chop the comice pears and sprinkle with lemon juice and cider vinegar. Leave to sit for 1 hour to allow the pears to pickle. Crumb the Stilton cheese in a bowl, using a wooden spoon, until smooth and creamy. Add the yoghurt, then the pickled pears, mixing well. Dissolve the gelatine in 1 tablesp. of water over gentle heat, then add to the cheese mixture. Using a spatula add the whisked egg white, chopping through to mix evenly. Transfer to individual ramekin dishes or dariole moulds.

Set in the fridge for 1 to 1½ hours, unmould, and garnish with lettuce, coriander leaves, and some pickled pears.

Warm Asparagus and Orange Salad

Medium-sized asparagus is suitable for this simple and delicious warm salad. The flavour of orange is infused into the light olive oil dressing.

20 long asparagus spears
Rind and juice of 1 orange
4 tablesp. light olive oil
2 tablesp. fresh thyme leaves

Trim the asparagus spears and steam until tender (5–7 minutes approximately). Grate the rind of the orange and squeeze the juice, then add it to the heated olive oil and the thyme leaves. Season to taste. Drain the asparagus spears, and spoon the dressing generously over them.

Serve with crusty bread, to dip into the dressing.

Serves 4

Lettuce Soup with Mint

This is bright green soup, thin in texture, with a rather speckled effect.

1 cos or butterhead lettuce
30 g (1 oz) butter
1 tablesp. oil
1 onion, coarsely chopped
1 potato, diced and tossed in a teasp. lemon juice
1.1 L (2 pints) chicken or vegetable stock
A few sprigs of mint

Sweat the onion and potato in the oil and butter, stirring occasionally, then replace the lid on the pot and leave for 5–6 minutes. Add the chicken stock and simmer for a further 5 minutes.

Remove the entire stalk from the lettuce and shred finely. Use preferably all the outer leaves, and add to the soup with the seasoning. Give a good stir to mix it well for 1–2 minutes, otherwise the bright colour of the soup will disappear, then liquidise.

Serve with a sprig of mint and a swirl of cream or yoghurt.

Serves 6

Geranium-Leaf Sorbet

The use of the lemon-scented cottage geranium, *Pelargonium graveolens*, gives this sorbet a delightfully light lemony flavour.

8–10 scented geranium leaves
85 g (3 oz) caster sugar
280 ml (½ pint) water
Juice of 1 lemon
1 egg white
Geranium or mint leaves to decorate

Wash the geranium leaves and shake them dry. Put the sugar and water in a pan and boil until the sugar has dissolved. Put the leaves in the pan, turn off the heat, and leave to infuse for 20 minutes, then taste; if the flavour is too weak, bring to the boil once more and leave for a further 10 minutes. Strain the syrup, add the lemon juice, and leave to cool. Freeze until semi-frozen (about 45 minutes to 1 hour), then fold in the stiffly beaten egg white. Continue to freeze until it is a firm mush (about 1 hour).

Serve in glasses, each one decorated with a tiny geranium or mint leaf.

Serves 4

Summer Dill Trout

Fish with herbs or herbs with fish—whichever way it was meant to be the herbs have a clever way of bringing out the best in fish.

1 trout, 1 kg (2 lb) approx.

Stuffing

115 g (4 oz) wholemeal breadcrumbs
Rind and juice of ½ lemon
30 g (1 oz) chopped almonds
4 dessertsp. chopped fresh dill
2 dessertsp. olive or grapeseed oil

To Bake

30 g (1 oz) unsaturated fat
Honey to baste

Bone the fish, then to the cavity add the stuffing, made by combining all the ingredients well together. Place in a microwave-proof dish, and cover with knobs of fat, black pepper, and honey, baking on high heat for 4–5 minutes. Alternatively the fish may be baked in the oven at 180 °C (350 °F or regulo 4) for 20–25 minutes.

Serve on a bed of lightly steamed green vegetables: green beans, celery, broccoli stalks, and fennel.

Salmon Under Wraps

Potato Pastry

285 g (10 oz) plain flour
140 g (5 oz) polyunsaturated fat
115 g (4 oz) cooked sieved potatoes

Filling

340 g (12 oz) fresh salmon
2 stalks dill or parsley
1 tablesp. lemon or lime juice
30 g (1 oz) butter
Egg wash to brush

Make the potato pastry by sieving the flour into a bowl, then cut and rub in the fat until the mixture resembles fine breadcrumbs. Add the cooked potato and use it to bind the pastry together. Knead well to remove any cracks, then roll out on a floured surface into a rectangle 300 by 200 mm (12 by 8 in.), making diagonal slits on the outer one-third edge on both sides. Brush the edges with egg wash.

Partly cook the salmon, either by poaching or in the microwave, for 3 minutes on full power. Flake the fish and add the chopped herbs and knobs of butter or fat to keep the fish moist during baking. Place the filling on the centre of the pastry and, using a spatula, carefully overlap the slit sides, being sure not to overlap the pastry, otherwise it will shrink during cooking. Brush with egg wash, garnish with pastry leaves, and bake at 220 °C (425 °F or regulo 7) for 25–30 minutes.

Mayonnaise Sauce

125 ml (4½ fl. oz) mayonnaise
½ chopped cucumber
½ teasp. paprika pepper
A few drops Tabasco sauce

Mix all the ingredients together and serve in a sauce boat.

Serves 4–5

New Potatoes with Lemon and Mint Dressing

450 g (1 lb) new potatoes, scrubbed
140 ml (5 fl. oz) sour cream
1 lemon rind, freshly grated
1 tablesp. fresh mint, finely chopped
Salt and freshly ground black pepper

Garnish

Sprigs of fresh mint
Lemon slices

Place the potatoes in lightly salted boiling water and cook until tender. Mix the sour cream, lemon rind and mint in a bowl; season to taste. Drain the potatoes, pour on the dressing and toss until well coated.

Garnish with fresh mint and lemon slices and serve immediately.

Orange, Watercress and Walnut Salad

3 oranges, segmented
85 g (3 oz) chopped walnuts
2 bunches watercress
1 tablesp. walnut oil

Mix the well-rinsed watercress, orange segments, walnuts and oil well together, and serve chilled.

French Beans with Hazelnut Dressing

French beans add a crisp sweetness, whether cooked by steaming or by plunging into boiling water for just a few minutes. Make sure they retain their crunch and colour.

450 g (1 lb) French beans, trimmed and cooked
140 ml (¼ pint) sour cream
3 tablesp. mayonnaise
115 g (4 oz) hazelnuts
Juice of ½ lemon
Lemon slices to garnish

Beat the sour cream and mayonnaise together until blended; add the lemon juice. Arrange the beans in a serving dish. Spoon the dressing over the beans, and sprinkle with roasted chopped hazelnuts.

Serves 4

Wild Strawberry Cake

30 g (1 oz) melted fat
1 tablesp. honey
115 g (4 oz) crushed oatmeal biscuits
½ teasp. cinnamon

Filling

225 g (8 oz) alpine strawberries
1 teasp. caster sugar
115 g (4 oz) low-fat strawberry yoghurt
140 ml (¼ pint) whipped cream
15 g (½ oz) dissolved gelatine

Prepare the base for a 200 mm (8 in.) loose-bottomed cake tin or, alternatively, a flan dish. Mix together the melted fat, honey, cinnamon, and crushed biscuits, then transfer to the tin and press down well, using a spoon (careful packing at this stage should make serving easier). Leave aside for at least 5–10 minutes to cool.

To make the filling, soften the strawberries by mixing lightly with a fork, and add a little caster sugar. Add to the fruit the yoghurt and whipped cream, mixing well. Add the dissolved gelatine to set the entire mixture, and when the pudding shows signs of setting, pour on top of the oatmeal base, and chill in the fridge for 1 to 1½ hours.

Decorate with wild strawberries and their leaves.

Serves 8–10

Rosie's Rhubarb in Ginger Beer

I called this recipe Rosie's rhubarb after my sister, who grew the most wonderful flavoured rhubarb in her own little vegetable garden which she called Cosy Corner.

3–4 stalks rhubarb
280 ml (½ pint) ginger beer
30 g (1 oz) demerara sugar

Place the ginger beer and sugar in a saucepan and dissolve over a gentle heat. Poach the fingers of rhubarb for approximately 5 minutes, being careful to keep the stalks of rhubarb firm in texture.

Serve chilled with ginger cream, which is simply whipped cream with the addition of a few pieces of crystallised ginger, finely chopped.

Serves 4

5. Time for Tea

Making a cup of tea is something we all do several times a day, but rarely do we take the time to stop what we are doing and sit down with a really good cup of tea and something delicious to eat. There is nothing more homely than a good afternoon tea sitting in front of a warm crackling fire with an abundance of home-baked food.

One of the best afternoon teas I ever had was as a child perched on top of a haystack. It was haymaking time, and I remember vividly the teapot with the spout plugged with newspaper to stop it spilling and to keep it warm on the journey from the house. I never wanted my tea first, just in case it tasted of newspaper; but it really did have a taste all of its own. I still remember piping hot tea scented with the smell of wild grass and meadow hay, and the sandwiches or 'pieces' made of thick white bread with the crusts left on and filled with the home jams and jellies. Rhubarb and ginger was never my favourite; I always hoped to find hidden in the depth of the basket the damson, crab-apple jelly, or—the most favoured—those filled with strawberry jam.

Happily, good afternoon tea is on the way back. Plenty of variety and plenty of everything is the key to success. I have included an old-fashioned gingerbread with walnuts. This gingerbread improves and matures if stored for several days to develop a rich dark moistness. Cinnamon toast is a great favourite and so simple to make.

The wholemeal scones can be served either with a sweet or savoury filling. Try apricot purée or cottage cheese with pineapple. And the whole secret of scone-making lies in the consistency of the dough. Make sure it is not too stiff or it will be difficult to work with.

For those with a sweet tooth, try dipping a sugar cube in lemon juice for just a few seconds, then press it into the top of the scones before baking. This creates a wonderfully sugary crust.

Chocolate cake has always been a favourite of mine, and the devilish dark chocolate is all that I expect a cake to be: dark, rich, moist, very good and very wicked.

The Irish apple cake is ideal for serving either warm or cold with a good dollop of yoghurt sweetened with a dessertspoon of runny honey.

Everyone has their own method of making a good cup of tea. Don't forget to warm the pot first, and don't overboil the water or reheat the tea more than once. The varieties of tea on the market are increasing by the day: herb teas, fruit teas, lemon, iced, Chinese or Indian—we all have our favourites.

Cinnamon Toast

6 slices wholemeal bread
2 teasp. demerara sugar
1 level teasp. cinnamon powder

Butter the bread and sprinkle with the mixed demerara sugar and cinnamon. Place below the grill for 1 to 2 minutes, then cut into finger slices and serve hot.

Wholemeal Scones

115 g (4 oz) wholemeal flour
½ teasp. baking powder
115 g (4 oz) self-raising flour
45 g (1½ oz) unsaturated fat
1 egg, lightly beaten
140 ml (¼ pint) milk
Pinch of salt

Sieve the flour and salt into a baking bowl, and add the wholemeal flour and baking powder. Mix well, then rub in the fat, and add the egg and sufficient milk to mix to a reasonably soft dough. Sprinkle the board with wholemeal flour, roll out to 25 mm (1 in.) thickness and cut out the scones. Brush with egg yolk and bake at 220 °C (425 °F or regulo 7) for 10–15 minutes.

As a savoury, serve with cottage cheese, cucumber, and prawns. As a sweet, serve with cottage cheese and apricot purée.

Herb Garden Bread

170 g (6 oz) wholemeal flour
30 g (1 oz) bran
30 g (1 oz) self-raising flour
30 g (1 oz) polyunsaturated fat
1 teasp. baking soda
280 ml (½ pint) approx. buttermilk

Filling

4 dessertsp. chopped parsley
2 dessertsp. marjoram
30 g (1 oz) polyunsaturated fat

Preheat the oven to 200 °C (400 °F or regulo 6). Sieve the self-raising flour into a bowl, and add the wholemeal flour, bran, and baking soda, mixing well. Cut in the fat, then, mixing well, add the buttermilk to the mix to make a soft but firm dough. Turn out onto a floured baking sheet and shape into a rectangle 150 by 200 mm (6 by 8 in.). Spread with the chopped herbs, mixed with a little fat. Roll up as for a swiss roll, and place in a round earthenware jar or 225 g (½ lb) loaf tin. Bake for 20–25 minutes.

Serves 6–8

Gooseberry Cake

170 g (6 oz) butter or unsaturated fat
170 g (6 oz) soft brown sugar
225 g (8 oz) self-raising flour
3 large eggs
Rind and juice of 1 orange
225 g (8 oz) small green gooseberries

Top and tail the gooseberries into a bowl. Cream the fat and sugar until light and fluffy, then alternately fold in the lightly beaten egg and flour, mixing well between each addition. Fold in the orange rind and juice and the lightly floured gooseberries.

Grease the base of a lined 200 mm (8 in.) spring-clip cake tin, then turn the mixture into the tin. Bake at 180 °C (350 °F or regulo 4) for 1 hour. Cool for a few minutes before unmoulding, then if desired decorate with whole gooseberries on top.

Serve this deliciously moist cake as a pudding while it is still warm, with plenty of cream.

Serves 8

Hearts and Tarts

225 g (8 oz) plain flour
2 teasp. cream of tartar
½ teasp. baking soda
½ teasp. salt
30 g (1 oz) caster sugar
30 g (1 oz) fat
1 egg, beaten
3–4 tablesp. milk

Sieve the plain flour, cream of tartar, baking soda, salt and caster sugar together. Cut and rub in the fat; add the beaten egg and 3–4 tablesp. milk to mix to a firm but soft dough. Roll the pastry out to a thickness of 10 mm (⅜ in.), then cut out half the quantity with a heart-shaped cutter and the remainder with a fluted pastry cutter, and place in a tartlet or patty tin. Prick lightly with a fork, then allow 10–15 minutes in the fridge to relax before baking at 160 °C (325 °F or regulo 3) for 10–15 minutes.

Decorate the heart-shaped biscuits with whipped cream and strawberries, and the tartlets with summer fruits to which have been added the rind and juice of half a lemon and an orange, and a sprig of apple mint.

Old-Fashioned Gingerbread with Walnuts

115 g (4 oz) fat, melted
115 g (4 oz) soft brown sugar
1 dessertsp. honey or syrup
1 dessertsp. treacle
170 g (6 oz) self-raising flour
55 g (2 oz) wholemeal flour
2 teasp. ginger powder
1 level teasp. mixed spice
55 g (2 oz) finely chopped walnuts
1 egg, whisked
70 ml (⅛ pint) milk

Melt the fat in a saucepan, then add the sugar, honey, and treacle. Stir well over gentle heat to dissolve the sugar. Sieve the self-raising flour into a bowl, add the wholemeal flour, ginger, mixed spice, and nuts, and add the egg to the milk (this will reduce the danger of curdling when you pour the egg-milk mixture into the flour after the treacle mixture). Mix well until it has a good smooth texture. Pour into a greased 225 g (½ lb) loaf tin, sprinkle with a few walnuts, and bake at 160 °C (325 °F or regulo 3) for 25 minutes or until firm to the touch.

Serves 8

Irish Apple Cake

85 g (3 oz) fat
85 g (3 oz) caster sugar
2 eggs
115 g (4 oz) self-raising flour
30 g (1 oz) ground almonds
Rind of ½ lemon
A few drops vanilla essence
2 eating apples

Apricot Glaze

2 tablesp. apricot jam, sieved
1 teasp. water

This cake is made by the traditional creaming method. Cream the fat and sugar until light and fluffy, then alternately add the lightly beaten egg and sieved flour in two additions, mixing well between each. Finally add the mixed almonds, lemon rind, and vanilla essence. Pour into a 200 mm (8 in.) greased tin, and flatten out the sponge mixture, which should come half-way up the sides of the tin. Place the wedges of apple into the sponge mixture, then bake at 190 °C (375 °F or regulo 5) for 15–20 minutes. The sponge mixture will rise and enclose the apples.

While still warm and when turned out onto a cooling tray, brush the top side with apricot glaze. Serve dusted with icing sugar.

Serves 8–10

Devilish Dark Chocolate Cake

200 g (7 oz) fat
200 g (7 oz) dark brown sugar
4 eggs
115 g (4 oz) self-raising flour
1 level teasp. baking powder
115 g (4 oz) chocolate powder
1 teasp. honey
Vanilla essence
1 dessertsp. milk

To Decorate

225 g (8 oz) chocolate (dark or milk)
30 g (1 oz) butter

Cream the fat and brown sugar until light and fluffy. Add lightly beaten eggs and the already sieved flour and baking powder; at this stage add also the chocolate powder and honey and a few drops of vanilla essence. Whisk all the ingredients together for at least 2 minutes. If the consistency is a little stiff, add 1 dessertsp. of milk. Transfer to a well-greased angel cake tin and bake at 190 °C (375 °F or regulo 5) for 30–35 minutes until firm to the touch. Melt the chocolate in the microwave or over a low heat, taking care not to overheat. Add the butter to the chocolate and beat well. Pour the melted chocolate over the cooled cake, being careful not to damp the knife before spreading the chocolate.

Decorate with redcurrants or seasonal fruits.

Serves 10

6. A Movable Feast

I always get excited about going on a picnic, whether it is a simple sandwiches-and-lemonade affair or a more elaborate feast. It's the fun of escaping out of doors, regardless of the planning or preparation required for a 'movable feast'. I admire the enthusiasm of one very good friend who says that when he plans a picnic he goes despite the weather, echoing exactly my feelings that picnicking is all about a sense of occasion. Living in an unpredictable climate, I have adapted many of my recipes to suit the weather.

Picnics usually involve a journey, no matter how short, and there never was an appetite that didn't improve in the open air. With informal parties such as picnics or barbecues there is such a relaxed air that I find that after the preparation of the food there are many eager helpers to take over the cooking and serving.

Food that can be eaten with the fingers is what you want. Make sure it will travel well, and aim for good, fresh ingredients balanced with simplicity. A good warming soup such as Broughdone broth is always welcome on arrival at your destination. This hot bacon and lentil soup is good served with the oatmeal muffins.

Patés, terrines—call them what you will—are excellent travelling food. They are easily served, spreadable, and dippable, and the texture can be so easily altered by the help of a good processor. This fish terrine with smoked haddock is also very good with the muffins or daily wholemeal bread.

The forester's pie just by its very ingredients creates a special occasion. This pie is quite time-consuming to make, but I believe is very well worth the effort. It is also good to have one substantial dish, especially if the weather is chilly. The hot-water crust pastry is easy to make and ideal for picnics.

Every picnic needs a good cake, and this picnic fruit cake meets the criteria that I expect of a fruit cake. It is made by an unusual method of lightly boiling the dried fruits, then allowing them to cool before adding them to an almost genoese sponge mixture made by the whisking method. Unlike most fruit cakes, this one does not need time to mature and tastes equally good if eaten the next day.

I find sandwiches an invaluable and very popular food for the ravenous children who like to eat on the move. On a picnic they discover more than just the immediate area, so don't forget to pack the insect bite cream and something for wasp sting. And if you have to forget something, don't let it be the corkscrew!

Speckled speedy griddle cakes.

Farmhouse casserole with potato and herb cobbler.

Braised mushroom dumplings with red-hot spicy sauce.

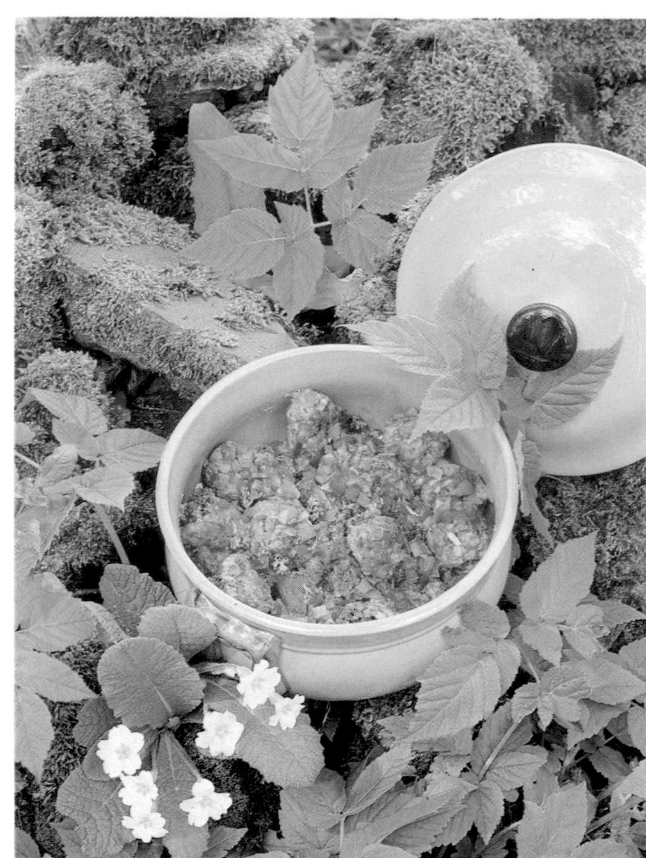

Honey, mustard and sugar glazed ham.

Camus cottage meatloaf.

Farmhouse pie.

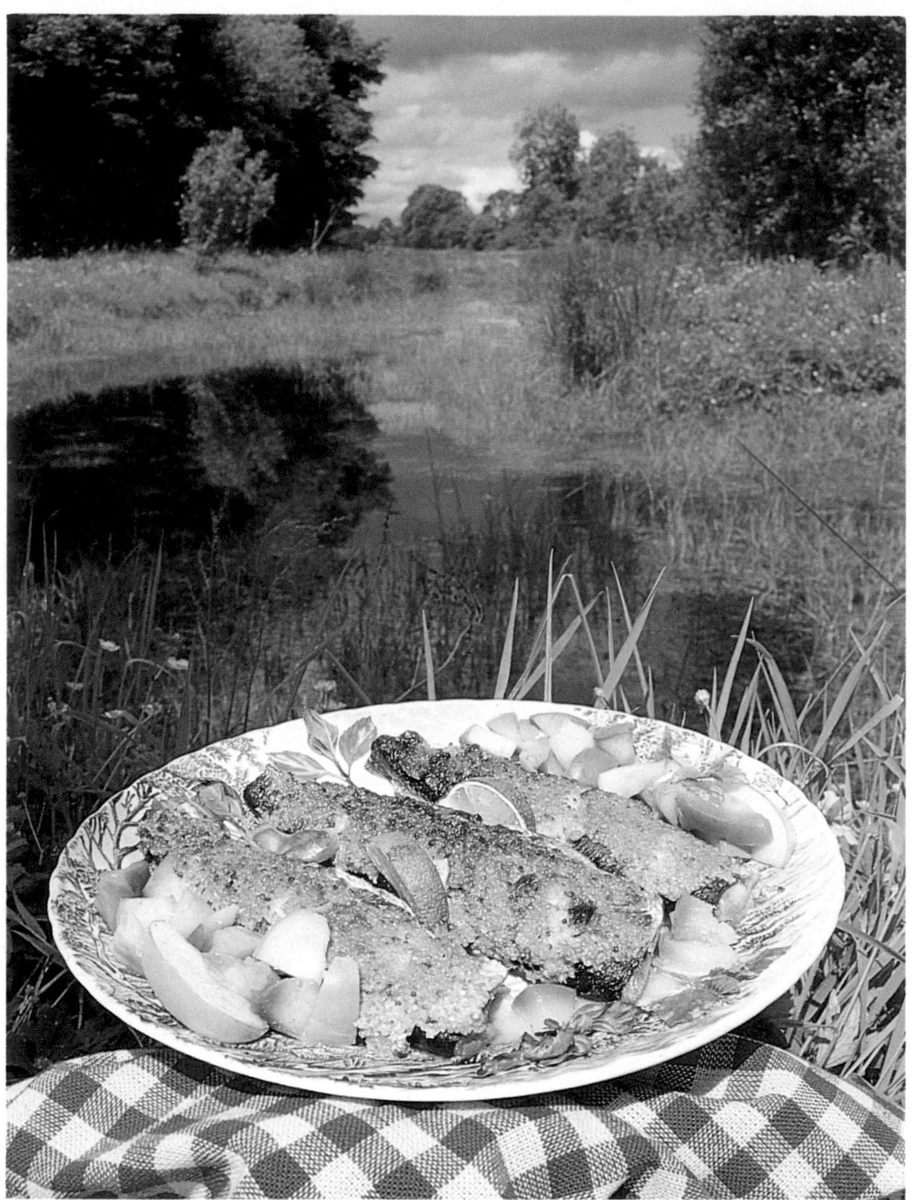

Grilled mackerel with cider sauce.

Baked potatoes and fillings.
Dinner party mince.

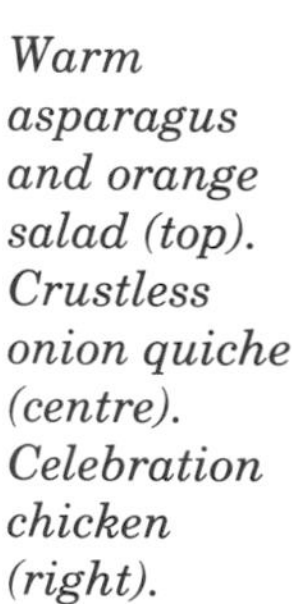

Warm asparagus and orange salad (top). Crustless onion quiche (centre). Celebration chicken (right).

Symphony of seafood in champagne sauce.

Ma King's salmon.

Garlicky chicken with a lemony sauce (top). Molly Malone's fish pie (bottom).

Travelling Terrine

425 ml (¾ pint) milk
1 bay leaf
2 peppercorns
450 g (1 lb) smoked haddock
225 g (8 oz) cooked spinach, lightly steamed

Sauce

45 g (1½ oz) fat
45 g (1½ oz) flour
425 ml (¾ pint) stock, used to cook fish
1 dessertsp. dill
2 spring onions, finely chopped
4 dessertsp. low-fat cheese
15 g (½ oz) prepared gelatine
2 egg whites

Poach the smoked haddock gently in the milk, bay leaf and peppercorns until just tender. Drain the cooked fish and use the stock in which it was cooked to make a sauce. Strain the liquid into a jug. Melt the fat in a pan, and add the flour and cooled liquid. Boil for 1 minute, then allow to cool. Add the flaked fish, dill, spring onions, cheese, and dissolved gelatine. Mix well, and fold in the 2 egg whites, which have been beaten to form stiff peaks.

Transfer half the fish mixture into a terrine dish, layer with cooked spinach and finally the remainder of the fish. Place in the fridge for 1 hour before serving, then garnish with lime and flat-leafed parsley.

Serves 8–10

Broughdone Broth

1 onion
115 g (4 oz) bacon
2 cloves of garlic
1 carrot
1 stick of celery
1 bay leaf
170 g (6 oz) green lentils
400 g (14 oz) tinned tomatoes
570 ml (1 pint) water

Lightly cook the bacon, onion and garlic in a pan. The fat on the bacon should give sufficient oil for frying. Cook for 1–2 minutes. To the soup add the finely diced carrot, celery, bay leaf, and green lentils, which have been boiled in salted water. Stir well, then place the lid on top and simmer gently for 30–35 minutes.

Oatmeal Muffins

3 eggs
6 dessertsp. melted butter
380 ml (⅔ pint) cold milk
½ cup fine oatmeal
½ teasp. salt
1½ cup self-raising flour

Whisk the eggs in a bowl, then add the melted butter (this can be melted in a microwave or in a saucepan). Add the cold milk and mix. Add the oatmeal, pinch of salt, and finally the self-raising flour. Mix well, then transfer to patty or muffin tin and bake at 200 °C (400 °F or regulo 6) for 20–25 minutes.

Makes 10–12 muffins

Forester's Pie

1 pheasant
1 pigeon
1 quail

Marinade

280 ml (½ pint) red wine
140 ml (¼ pint) olive oil
2 dessertsp. parsley
1 teasp. sage
1 teasp. rosemary
Pinch of salt
3 cloves of garlic
A few juniper berries
225 g (8 oz) mushrooms
225 g (8 oz) streaky bacon
30 g (1 oz) butter

Hot-Water Crust Pastry

170 ml (6 fl. oz) water
115 g (4 oz) butter
115 g (4 oz) lard or unsaturated fat
450 g (1 lb) flour
1 egg yolk
1 teasp. salt

Stock

Bones of pigeon, pheasant, quail
1 carrot, 1 onion, 1 celery stalk (chopped)
1 bay leaf
570 ml (1 pint) water
15 g (½ oz) gelatine
Seasoning

First bone the game birds carefully, removing the flesh from the breasts and legs with a sharp knife. Cut the meat into 12 mm (½ in.) strips. Place the bones in a roasting tin with 1 carrot, 1 onion, a little salt and pepper, celery, and 570 ml (1 pint) water and roast for ½ hour. Cool, then strain the stock through muslin.

Make the marinade by mixing all the ingredients together: red wine, olive oil, herbs, and seasoning. Pour the marinade over the birds in three separate bowls, and leave to sit in a covered vessel, preferably overnight. Fry the birds in 30 g (1 oz) melted butter, keeping the flesh separate, for 3–5 minutes. In another pan cook the mushrooms and streaky bacon in 30 g (1 oz) fat for 1–2 minutes. Do not overcook at this stage, as the filling will be cooked within the pastry.

To Make the Pastry

This quantity makes enough to line a 1.4 L (2½ pint) mould or 200 mm (8 in.) cake tin.

Warm a mixing bowl and sieve the flour and salt into it. Make a well in the centre and hide the egg in the flour. Heat the butter, lard and water in a saucepan, and when boiling make sure that the fat has melted before boiling point is reached. Pour into the flour and egg, mixing well with a spoon or knife. When the dough has cooled slightly turn onto a floured surface and knead until the pastry is smooth. It is a good idea to cover the pastry with cling film and leave it to rest at this stage for 15–20 minutes. Then use two-thirds to line the dish (keeping one-third for the topping), pressing the pastry firmly into the tin.

Pack the cooked meats well into the tin, layering pheasant, pigeon, quail, bacon, and mushrooms, and a sprinkling of parsley; repeat the process. The stock can be thickened with 15 g (½ oz) gelatine and poured over the pie at this stage if a very moist pie is preferred. Brush the top of the pastry with beaten egg, place the rolled-out third of pastry on top, and, using fingers, seal well on top. Decorate with pastry leaves, and make a hole to allow the steam to escape. Bake at 190 °C (375 °F or regulo 5) for 30–35 minutes.

Serves 12–14

Crustless Onion Quiche

This is a very easy and quick dish that does not involve the making and rolling out of pastry. A variety of fillings can be used, but in this onion quiche I have combined flavours by adding cooked chopped bacon and mushrooms.

170 g (6 oz) plain flour
55 g (2 oz) bran
6 eggs
¼ teasp. salt
85 g (3 oz) unsaturated margarine
425 ml (1 pint) milk
2 large onions, finely chopped
115 g (4 oz) mushrooms
170 g (6 oz) finely chopped bacon
115 g (4 oz) grated cheese to flavour and garnish

Sieve the flour and salt into a large bowl, then rub in the margarine. Add the bran. Whisk the eggs, milk and cheese and add, mixing well, along with the bacon and mushrooms. Thoroughly grease a 250 mm (10 in.) quiche dish, then, mixing well, pour the mixture into the dish and bake in the middle shelf of a preheated oven at 180 °C (350 °F or regulo 4) for 30 minutes or until golden-brown and well risen. Cut, and serve either hot or cold.

Serves 10

Picnic Fruit Cake

170 g (6 oz) raisins
170 g (6 oz) glacé cherries, cut in half
30 g (1 oz) glacé pineapple
115 g (4 oz) dried chopped apricots
55 g (2 oz) chopped hazelnuts
30 g (1 oz) chopped almonds
2 tablesp. water
2 tablesp. dark rum
4 eggs
115 g (4 oz) soft brown sugar
115 g (4 oz) softened butter
140 g (5 oz) self-raising flour
55 g (2 oz) ground almonds
1 teasp. mixed spice

Prepare the fruit by adding the raisins, cherries, pineapple, apricots, hazelnuts and almonds to a saucepan in which the water and dark rum have been warmed. Stir the fruit well, turn off the heat, place the lid on top, and leave to cool completely. This should take 15–20 minutes.

When cool, beat the eggs in a separate bowl until stiff and forming a figure-of-eight shape, add the brown sugar, and mix well. Next add the softened butter, mixing well; then carefully fold in the self-raising flour. Finally add the ground almonds and mixed spice and fruit, making sure the fruit is evenly mixed. Transfer to a lined 175 mm (7 in.) cake tin and bake at 180 °C (350 °F or regulo 4) for 1½ hours on the middle shelf.

7. Happy Christmas

Christmas has to be the highday and most magical holiday of the entire year, and isn't Christmas dinner the culmination of all those endless hours of planning, preparation, and shopping! It's a time for food, family, feasting, and friends, all of which have been an important part of the Christmas tradition.

The ingredients for Christmas have changed little over the years, but whatever we eat it's all about the determination to be organised well in advance (not like last year!) and to prepare, cook and serve something just that little bit more special to those we care for.

Christmas is my favourite time of the year. I just love all the planning and shopping, the cooking and entertaining, which appears to start earlier every year. In our home Christmas starts when on go the boots and off we go to gather the holly, the spruce and the ivy for the Christmas decorations.

Every year I try to give Christmas dinner just that different touch. For example, clementine sorbet, a light, refreshing starter served with an unusual fruit cocktail, can be made weeks in advance and stored in the freezer.

Winter parsnip and roasted chestnut soup—doesn't the very name sound Christmassy? Again this can be made in advance and it also freezes well, and the roasted chestnuts give this soup a special flavour.

Christmas wouldn't be Christmas without the turkey, the most traditional food eaten in homes at Christmas time. Try filling the cavity with only a lemon, orange, and bunch of herbs; this allows air to circulate around the bird, allowing it to cook more evenly and giving a very moist turkey on serving. Only stuff the neck of the bird; and if extra stuffing is required cook it in a separate dish in the oven.

When it comes to the vegetables I like just a little of everything. Try serving a platter of baby vegetables for a change, and if these are difficult to obtain or expensive, then slice the bigger ones into shorter lengths.

Christmas morning cranberry muffins, combining all those festive aromas of orange, cranberries, cinnamon, and nuts, are a nice alternative to mince pies for those friends who just drop in.

I always make a chocolate yule log. It is very light and easy to roll.

The smell of the Christmas cake baking in the oven is so much part of the preparation! My two-fruit Christmas cake is very economical to make and a light alternative to the traditional cake, but, like most Christmas cakes, it improves on maturing. If time is running out, however, try wrapping the cake in tinfoil and placing it in the freezer for 6–7 days. This speeds up the maturing process.

Just remember that when it's time for cake on Christmas Day all the work and effort will have been worth while, so sit back and enjoy it, realising that you have at least twenty-four hours to work out what to do with the leftovers!

Mulled Wine

1.7 L (3 pints) water
225 g (8 oz) granulated sugar
2–3 cinnamon sticks
3 oranges
10–12 cloves
2 bottles red wine
1 apple and orange to serve

Roughly cut up the oranges and place in a saucepan with all the other ingredients, except for the red wine. Heat gently until the sugar has dissolved, then bring to the boil, simmer for 30 minutes, and strain. (The syrup can be made up to this stage and then stored in the fridge until required.)

To serve, return the syrup to the pan, bring to boiling point, add the wine and slice of apple and orange, and serve.

Serves 10–12

Cranberry Muffins

1 cup cranberries
¼ cup brown demerara sugar
1½ cups self-raising flour
¼ cup white sugar
1 teasp. baking powder
½ teasp. salt
½ teasp. cinnamon
¼ teasp. nutmeg
1 beaten egg
½ teasp. grated orange peel
¼ cup freshly squeezed orange juice
⅓ cup melted butter or margarine
¼ cup chopped walnuts

Coarsely chop the cranberries, sprinkle with brown sugar, and set aside. In a bowl stir together the flour, white sugar, baking powder, salt, cinnamon, and spice, and make a well in the centre. Combine the egg, orange peel, orange juice, and melted butter; add all the moist ingredients, and mix well. Fold in the cranberries and nuts. Fill the greased muffin cups and bake for 15–20 minutes at 190 °C (375 °F or regulo 5).

Serve warm, dusted with icing sugar and cinnamon.

Makes 12 muffins

Clementine Sorbet

This starter with a pure fruit flavour and an icy smooth texture combines well with a seasonal fruit cocktail.

280 ml (½ pint) clementine orange juice
85 g (3 oz) caster sugar
Rind of ½ lemon
1 egg white

Fruit Cocktail

2 grapefruit
2 clementine oranges
2 mandarin oranges
Other options: melon, kumquats, cape gooseberries

Add the caster sugar to the freshly squeezed orange juice and lemon rind, bring to the boil, and simmer for approximately 10 minutes. Pour into a bowl and place in the freezer to set. This usually takes about 1 hour.

When it is firm, add 1 well-beaten egg white to the sorbet, using a gentle folding action. Return the mixture to the freezer. (The sorbet can be made to this stage weeks in advance and stored in the freezer until required.)

Serve on its own in pretty glasses or with the fruit cocktail around the outside. Garnish with mint.

Serves 6

Winter Parsnip and Roasted Chestnut Soup

Here is a soup where the flavours of the faintly sweet parsnips combines beautifully with that of the chestnut. This soup also freezes extremely well.

2 onions
1 tablesp. cooking oil
900 g (2 lb) parsnips
Salt
Freshly milled pepper
1–1.75 L (2–3 pints) chicken or vegetable stock
225 g (½ lb) chestnuts approx. (when prepared)
Swirl of cream to garnish

Cook the finely chopped onions in a large pan in a little oil. Add the small diced parsnips, coat well in the oil, then add the salt, pepper, and freshly squeezed root ginger. Put the lid on the pan, reduce the temperature, and cook for 15–20 minutes, stirring occasionally. Then add the stock and leave to simmer for a further 30 minutes or until the vegetables are sufficiently soft to liquidise or push through a sieve.

When sieved add half of the roasted chestnuts to the soup, and stir. I find the way to get most flavour from the chestnuts is to make a slit on the flat side of their shells, from the centre to the pointed end. Place in cold water to cover, and bring to the boil. Simmer for 4–5 minutes, then when the chestnuts are still hot remove the shell and inner membrane. The shells come off easily if the chestnuts are hot but not overcooked.

Place the chestnuts on a baking sheet and roast in the oven for 10–15 minutes at 200 °C (400 °F or regulo 6). Chop up very finely.

Serve the soup hot with a little swirl of cream and a good sprinkling of roasted chestnuts.

Serves 8–10

Christmas Turkey

I prefer the flavour of a fresh turkey. If you are using a frozen bird it is important to make sure it is completely thawed before cooking. Wipe the turkey inside and out before stuffing it.

Do not wash the turkey or the skin may not crisp. Stuff the neck loosely with your chosen stuffing. The stuffing is important to keep the turkey moist and to add flavour. The inside may not cook properly if the cavity is stuffed, so allow air to circulate inside by placing only a lemon or orange and a bunch of herbs in the cavity. This also improves the flavour and moisture.

Weigh the bird to calculate the cooking time. There are many ways of roasting a turkey, but I find it best to start it in a hot oven to seal the juices at 220 °C (425 °F or regulo 7) for 30 minutes, then reduce to 180 °C (350 °F or regulo 4) for the remainder of the cooking time, allowing 1 hour per kilogram (30 minutes per pound) plus 15 minutes standing time when removed from the oven. Stranding the turkey with bacon, and basting, help to keep the moisture in the bird during cooking.

Bread Stuffing with Lemon and Herbs

200–300 g (7–10 oz) white breadcrumbs
1 onion lightly fried in 30 g (1 oz) of butter
½ cup parsley
1 egg, lightly beaten
½ rind of lemon
½ rind of orange
1 teasp. spice
¼ teasp. nutmeg
A little melted fat to bind stuffing

To the fine breadcrumbs add onion, parsley, egg, spices, seasoning, and melted fat. Mix well and place in the neck of the bird.

Cranberry and Quince Sauce

225 g (8 oz) cranberries
3–4 quince apples
30 g (1 oz) demerara sugar
70 ml (⅛ pint) lemon juice

Place the cranberries and the peeled and sliced apples in a saucepan with the sugar and lemon juice. Bring to the boil, then simmer for 8–10 minutes. Serve hot.

Stir-Fry Sprouts with Hazelnuts

450 g (1 lb) brussels sprouts
115 g (4 oz) hazelnuts
1 dessertsp. cooking oil

Prepare the sprouts and cook in boiling water for only 1 minute. Drain, then place in a pan and stir-fry in the oil with the hazelnuts. Toss for 1–2 minutes, then serve hot.

Roast Sesame Potatoes

450 g (1 lb) small peeled potatoes
1 dessertsp. flour
A little beaten egg
115 g (4 oz) sesame seeds

Lightly boil the potatoes, then place on a roasting tin, brush with beaten egg, dust lightly with flour, and sprinkle liberally with sesame seeds. Roast in the oven, covering and basting occasionally with hot fat or oil.

Serve hot and crispy brown.

Honey, Mustard and Sugar Glazed Ham

This is one of the most traditional and flavoursome ways of cooking a ham. The juices are used to baste and flavour the ham while it is baking in the oven.

1 ham (unsmoked)
1 onion, peeled and studded with a few cloves
A few bay leaves
280 ml (½ pint) dry cider
Cold water to cover the ham

Glaze

4 tablesp. prepared English mustard
4 tablesp. honey
6 tablesp. demerara or soft brown sugar
Cloves to stud
150–300 ml (¼–½ pint) cider to bake

Place the ham in a large saucepan that will take it comfortably, and cover with cold water. Add an onion studded with cloves, cider, and bay leaves. Bring to the boil and simmer gently for 1–2 hours, depending on the size—I cook a 3 kg (7 lb) ham in water for 1½ hours.

Remove the ham and cool slightly, then, using a sharp knife, score the fat diagonally, first in one direction then the other, creating a diamond-shaped pattern. Mix the mustard and honey together and, using either your hands or a flat-bladed knife, spread the mixture over the top of the ham. Stud each diamond shape with a clove, and sprinkle with brown sugar, patting down well.

Transfer the ham to a roasting tin, pour the cider over it, and bake at 180 °C (350 °F or regulo 4) for ½ to 1 hour, basting occasionally.

Allow to brown well before serving.

Serves 12–14

Jenny's Plum Pudding

450 g (1 lb) butter
450 g (1 lb) soft brown sugar
6 eggs, lightly whisked
225 g (8 oz) plain flour
1 teasp. baking powder
225 g (8 oz) white breadcrumbs
450 g (1 lb) raisins
450 g (1 lb) sultanas
225 g (8 oz) glacé cherries
1 grated apple
Rind of 1 orange or lemon
Juice of ½ orange and ½ lemon
½ teasp. nutmeg
½ teasp. ground cloves
70 ml (½ gill) brandy

Cream the butter and sugar until light and fluffy, then alternately add the eggs, flour and breadcrumbs in two or three additions. Mix well before adding the fruits, spices, and grated apple, and finally the juice of the orange and lemon and the brandy, stirring well.

Because it is so light, this pudding can be steamed in a pudding basin, and you may find this an easier and more successful method. To make it in the old-fashioned cannonball shape, wring out two pieces of cotton in boiling water, and lay both pieces of cloth flat on the table, one on top of the other. Dust well with flour and pile the pudding into the centre of the cloth; gather in the corners, and tie them securely with string. To make sure that the pudding does not touch the bottom of the pot while steaming (thus ruining the shape) tie the pudding to the upturned lid and place this over the pot. Steam for 3½–4 hours.

Reheat on Christmas morning by steaming for a further hour, and serve hot with brandy sauce.

Serves 14–16

Brandy Sauce

This sauce is also very good over vanilla ice cream.

115 g (4 oz) melted butter
115 g (4 oz) soft brown sugar
1 egg, lightly whisked
140 ml (¼ pint) brandy
280 ml (½ pint) lightly whipped cream

Melt the butter in a saucepan, add the brown sugar, and stir until dissolved, cooking for 3–4 minutes. Allow to cool slightly, then add the beaten egg and brandy. Mix well. (This mixture can be stored in a screw-top jar in the fridge.) To complete the sauce, reheat the brandy mixture and add the lightly whipped cream. Serve warm.

Christmas Mincemeat

This simple-to-make mincemeat can be used for a variety of dishes, and for lovely home-made Christmas presents, such as mince pies, luxurious mincemeat flan, and mincemeat strudel.

225 g (8 oz) currants
225 g (8 oz) raisins
225 g (8 oz) sultanas
225 g (8 oz) soft brown sugar
225 g (8 oz) cooking apples, finely chopped
170 g (6 oz) grated or shredded beef suet
55 g (2 oz) walnuts
55 g (2 oz) blanched almonds
225 g (8 oz) whole mixed candied peel
Juice and grated rind of 2 oranges
Juice and grated rind of 1 lemon
1 teasp. cinnamon
1 grated nutmeg
½ teasp. cloves
4 tablesp. brandy

Wash and thoroughly dry the raisins, currants, and sultanas. Chop the walnuts and almonds finely. Wash, core and chop the apples (I like to leave the skin on). Grate the lemon and oranges and squeeze the juice. Chop the candied peel very finely. Combine all the ingredients except the brandy in a large bowl and mix well; cover the bowl and leave overnight to allow the flavours to develop. Add brandy before packing into clean, dry jars.

This mincemeat should store for 4–6 weeks if the jars are sterilised, but if you want the mincemeat to keep longer, perhaps to the following year, then its keeping qualities are greatly improved if you put the mincemeat into the oven in a large ovenproof bowl at the lowest setting for 2 hours. Add the brandy on cooling, then pack into clean, dry jars and seal. Store in a dark cupboard.

Mince Pies

285 g (10 oz) plain flour
55 g (2 oz) ground almonds
170 g (6 oz) butter
55 g (2 oz) icing sugar, sifted
Grated rind of ½ lemon
1 egg yolk
3–4 teasp. lemon juice
450 g (1 lb) mincemeat
A little milk

Mix the flour and almonds in a bowl. Cut and rub in the butter; add the sugar and lemon rind. Mix the egg yolk, lemon juice and milk to form a soft dough. Knead lightly, then chill for half an hour until firm. Roll out the pastry and make the mince pies. Bake at 180 °C (350 °F or regulo 4) for 15–20 minutes. Cool in the tins before trying to lift out the mince pies. Dust with icing or caster sugar.

This pastry is also good for making a larger mincemeat flan, which can be really spiced up for Christmas.

Two-Fruit Christmas Cake

680 g (1½ lb) sultanas
450 g (1 lb) glacé cherries (red, green, and yellow)
225 g (8 oz) plain flour
Pinch of salt
225 g (8 oz) butter
225 g (8 oz) soft brown sugar
4 eggs (size 2)
Rind of ½ lemon
30 g (1 oz) sliced whole almonds
55 g (2 oz) ground almonds
1 teasp. mixed spice
A little milk

Clean the sultanas by washing and drying well. Wash and chop the cherries in half, and dry well. Toss the cherries in one-third of the flour to be used in the recipe. Cream the butter and soft brown sugar until light and fluffy, then alternately add the lightly beaten eggs, flour, and almonds, in three additions. (Always sieve the flour before adding.) Add the lemon rind and mixed spice, and finally the sultanas and cherries; use a little milk to adjust the consistency. Transfer to a well-lined 230 mm (9 in.) cake tin and bake at 180 °C (350 °F or regulo 4) for half an hour. Reduce to 150 °C (300 °F or regulo 2) until cooked (approximately 1½ hours) or until a skewer is dry when removed from the cake.

Figgy Loaf Cake

140 g (5 oz) dried figs
1 tea-bag
1 teasp. orange juice
115 g (4 oz) fat
115 g (4 oz) soft brown sugar
2 eggs
115 g (4 oz) self-raising flour
85 g (3 oz) toasted walnuts
115 g (4 oz) sultanas
Rind of ½ orange

This cake can be made either in a loaf tin or a round loose-bottomed tin (make sure the tin is well lined and lightly greased). Toast the walnuts in the oven for 5 minutes. Into a bowl place the figs, tea-bag, and orange juice, and cover with boiling water. Allow to infuse for 15–20 minutes, then strain. Beat the fat and sugar together until soft and fluffy, then alternately fold in the eggs and flour. Add the toasted walnuts, sultanas, orange rind, and drained figs. Mix well, then transfer to the lined tin and bake at 180 °C (350 °F or regulo 4) for approximately 1 hour. Allow to cool slightly before turning out.

Serves 8

Marvellous Marble Cake

This is yet another of my favourite cakes. I love the marbled effect, and it is very easy to do.

170 g (6 oz) fat
170 g (6 oz) caster sugar
3 eggs
85 g (3 oz) self-raising flour
85 g (3 oz) ground almond
A few drops of almond and vanilla essence
Rind of ½ lemon
4 tablesp. cocoa powder

Lemony Icing
115 g (4 oz) caster sugar
Juice of 1 lemon

Beat together the fat and sugar until light, creamy, and fluffy. In a separate bowl whisk the eggs, then add to the creamed fat and sugar, mixing alternately with the flour and ground almonds to prevent the mixture curdling. Add the vanilla and almond essence and the lemon rind, and mix well. Divide the mixture into two separate bowls; to one add the sieved cocoa powder, then add the chocolate mixture and the lemony mixture to a lightly greased 1.1 L (2 pint) mould, swirling as you add it. Smooth the top, and bake at 180 °C (350 °F or regulo 4) for 1 hour. Allow to cool in the tin before turning it out.

I like to pour lemony icing over the top of this cake. To make this icing, boil the sugar in the lemon juice and when almost dissolved, turn off the heat and leave it aside to cool. Then paint it on the top and sides of the cake.

Serves 10

Tic-Tac-Toe Cake

This is a cake that was always made in our home at Christmas. It keeps very well if stored in an airtight tin—just the sort of stand-by cake useful at this time. (This recipe uses cupfuls, so the size of the cup will affect the overall volume.)

4 eggs
2½ cups caster sugar
1 cup butter
2½ cups plain flour
2 teasp. baking powder
1 cup sweet milk
First part: ½ cup raisins, ½ cup currants, ½ teasp. cinnamon
Second part: 2 tablesp. grated chocolate
Third part: ½ teasp. lemon flavouring and rind of ½ lemon

Sieve the flour and baking powder together until light and fluffy, then alternately fold in the slightly beaten eggs and melted butter; add the milk and mix lightly together (this is quite a soft mixture). Divide into three parts in three separate bowls. To the first add the currants, raisins, and cinnamon, and mix well. To the second add the grated chocolate, and mix well. To the third add the lemon rind and flavouring. Place the first part into the bottom of a well-lined 230 mm (9 in.) round tin, then add 1 spoonful of each of the two remaining bowls, going round in a circle until used. Bake for 45–50 minutes at 180 °C (350 °F or regulo 4).

Serves 10–12

Festive Chocolate Yule Log

This is my favourite version of chocolate log. Christmas is the time when a little indulgence is allowed without feeling too guilty, and this log rolls up so easily. There are endless ways to decorate it.

170 g (6 oz) plain chocolate
140 g (5 oz) caster sugar
55 g (2 oz) plain flour
5 eggs, separated

To Decorate

570 ml (1 pint) cream
1 tablesp. rum or brandy
115 g (4 oz) chopped nuts

Line a swiss roll tin with well-oiled greaseproof paper, snipping well into the corners. The size of tin used will affect the thickness of the chocolate log, but approximately 230 by 330 mm (9 by 13 in.) is a good size. If the log is too thick it will be difficult to roll.

Melt the chocolate in a Pyrex bowl over a pan of warm water. Be careful not to overheat the chocolate. In a separate bowl beat the egg yolks with the sugar until thick and creamy. In another bowl beat the egg whites until very stiff. To the egg yolk mixture add the melted chocolate and flour, and finally fold in the egg whites. Pour into the swiss roll tin and bake at 180 °C (350 °F or regulo 4) for 12–14 minutes. When cooked and firm to touch turn out onto a piece of greaseproof paper sprinkled with caster or icing sugar. Roll up and leave to cool.

I like to decorate the log by filling it with whipped cream and nuts and dusting with icing sugar on the outside. You can then add festive decorations or perhaps a little seasonal greenery.

Serves 8–10

Meringue Snowmen

3 egg whites
170 g (6 oz) caster sugar
140 ml (¼ pint) whipped cream
Hats, sweets, liquorice to decorate

Make up the meringue mixture: beat the egg whites with half the sugar until the mixture forms stiff peaks. Fold in the remainder of the sugar, transfer to a piping bag, and pipe out three rounds for each snowman, in assorted sizes: one for a head and two for a body. Bake at 150 °C (300 °F or regulo 2) for 1 hour, then cool and sandwich together and decorate.

8. For Your Heart's Sake

It used to be said that the way to a man's heart is through his stomach, but all too often it was the way to his heart attack; and yet most people today still have a reluctance to face the responsibilities of eating for their hearts' sake. But by only simple changes we can create for ourselves and our families a healthier way of life.

We all know we should cut down on our intake of fat, sugar, and salt, increase the amount of fibre, and eat more mineral and vitamin-related foods. It only takes the simplest of changes in shopping and in ways of cooking to produce easy, sensible meals that are full of good, wholesome food that can be eaten with enjoyment and satisfaction.

With these thoughts very much in my mind I put together a selection of dishes that not only taste good but are healthy, wholesome, and heartsome.

Molly Malone's Fish Pie

Everyone loves a good fish pie, and this one can be more economical, using varieties of fish such as coley or whiting. I like to use haddock; and with this recipe you can add a sense of occasion by the use of a few prawns, cockles, and mussels. This dish can be altered to serve as a first course, in individual ramekin dishes or scallop shells. The sauce could also be made using fromage frais as an alternative.

680 g (1½ lb) haddock, filleted and skinned
450 g (1 lb) cooked mashed potato
225 g (8 oz) mushrooms
1 leek
1 dessertsp. chopped parsley
Juice of ½ lemon and ½ lime
1 onion
1 dessertsp. olive oil

Sauce

30 g (1 oz) plain flour
30 g (1 oz) wholemeal flour
30 g (1 oz) polyunsaturated fat
140 ml (¼ pint) white fish stock
425 ml (¾ pint) semi-skimmed milk
Pinch of mustard

Optional

170 g (6 oz) prawns
A few mussels and cockles

Remove the skin, and cut the fish into equal good-sized pieces. Place in a bowl and add the lemon and lime juice and a little chopped parsley or dill. Boil the potatoes until just tender; the addition of some herbs helps to reduce the need for salt. Drain, shake the pan well to dry the potatoes, and mash with the milk and nutmeg. Transfer to a piping bag.

To make the filling, melt the fat in a large saucepan, gently toss the onion for about 2–3 minutes, and add the leek. Stir in the flour, stock, and milk, bringing to the boil. Add the cubes of fish, and the mushrooms, which can be lightly tossed in olive oil and microwaved for 30 seconds before adding. Cook for 4–5 minutes. If using them, add the cooked peeled prawns, mussels, and cockles. Transfer to a pie dish, and pipe the potatoes on top. Sprinkle with cheese and bake at 200 °C (400 °F or regulo 6) for 20–25 minutes.

Serve piping hot with a bowl of salad.

Serves 4–6

Grilled Mackerel with Cider Sauce

4 mackerel
4 teasp. coarse-grained mustard
Juice and rind of 1 lemon
30 g (1 oz) pinhead oatmeal
1 red apple, diced
1 green apple, diced
2 tablesp. water

Cut the heads off the mackerel. Mix the mustard, oatmeal and half the lemon juice together and rub over the mackerel fillets. Grill the mackerel for 4–5 minutes on both sides.

To make the cider sauce, simmer the apples, water and juice of half a lemon until just softening, then serve with the grilled mackerel (I like this sauce a little crunchy). Garnish with dill, and serve hot.

Crunchy Coleslaw

This is a combination of crisp raw vegetables in a lightly tossed dressing of orange juice and honey. It would make a very healthy light lunch if served with the buttermilk and oaten loaf.

55 g (2 oz) white cabbage, shredded
55 g (2 oz) carrots, peeled and cut into thin strips or shredded
55 g (2 oz) parsnips, peeled and cut into thin strips and grated
55 g (2 oz) cucumber
200 g (7 oz) can of sweet corn, drained
115 g (4 oz) black grapes, halved and seeded
55 g (2 oz) sultanas

Dressing

Juice of ½ freshly squeezed orange
1 dessertsp. runny honey

Alternative Dressing

1 carton natural low-fat yoghurt
1 dessertsp. runny honey

Mix the dressing ingredients together in a large bowl. Add the prepared salad ingredients to the dressing, tossing gently until well coated. Serve with a few chopped chives.

Serves 6

Garlicky Chicken with a Lemony Sauce

4 chicken breasts
2 cloves of garlic
1 bunch of spring onions
1 dessertsp. olive or sunflower oil
1 dessertsp. tarragon vinegar
1 dessertsp. honey
A few drops of soy sauce
340 g (12 oz) mushrooms, button or flat

Lemon Sauce

½ cup lemon juice
2 chicken stock cubes
2 tablesp. cornflour
2 tablesp. honey
1 tablesp. brown sugar
1 teasp. grated ginger
375 ml (1½ cups) water
Rind of 1 lemon
225 g (8 oz) filo pastry
Sesame seeds
A little beaten egg or oil to brush

Cut the chicken breasts into strips, then marinate in the crushed garlic, oil, tarragon vinegar, honey, and soy sauce; leave covered for 1–2 hours (longer if possible). Heat the olive oil in a pan and quickly fry the chicken pieces for 9–10 minutes until golden-brown; alternatively, the chicken pieces can be cooked in the microwave. Pour into an ovenproof dish. A few wild mushrooms could also be added.

To make the lemon sauce, combine the lemon juice, crumbled stock cubes, cornflour, honey, brown sugar, ginger, water and lemon rind in a saucepan, and stir over low heat until the sauce boils and thickens. Cut the spring onions into 25 mm (1 in.) pieces and add to the sauce, and pour it over the chicken pieces. Arrange the filo pastry on top of the pie; fold it into triangular pieces, and brush with a little beaten egg or oil or melted fat. Sprinkle with sesame seeds and bake at 220 °C (425 °F or regulo 7) for 25–30 minutes.

Serve with fresh salad, such as julienne of carrots and parsnips.

Serves 6

Hearty Game Hot Pot

Chicken, turkey, rabbit, pigeon, venison and pheasant are some of the meats with a low fat content. In this recipe I have used venison, lightly marinated and cooked by braising to give a very tasty casserole. The use of the low-fat meats creates a wider choice of menus.

680 g (1½ lb) good stewing venison, and flour to toss
450 g (1 lb) mushrooms
1 dessertsp. olive oil
4–5 stalks of celery tossed in lemon juice
140 ml (¼ pint) marinade (half dry red wine or red wine vinegar and half water)
570 ml (1 pint) good vegetable stock
2 bay leaves
1 large onion
Wholemeal garlicky croutons and parsley to serve

Soak the chunks of venison in the marinade and bay leaves for 6–12 hours (the longer the time allowed the more tender the venison will be to cook). Drain the venison and toss in the flour, then lightly cook in the hot oil. Transfer to an ovenproof casserole, and add the lightly cooked onion (this can be tossed in hot oil either before or after cooking the venison). Add the marinade, the stock, chunks of celery tossed in lemon juice, and bay leaf. Put a lid on top and braise in the oven at 180 °C (350 °F or regulo 4) for 1½–2 hours. Before serving add the lightly cooked mushrooms, and return to the oven for a further 15 minutes.

Serve sprinkled with wholemeal croutons and plenty of freshly chopped parsley and with baked dinner jacket potatoes.

Serves 6

Chicken and Celery Casserole with Mangoes

2 chicken breasts, skinned, boned, and cut into strips
1 teasp. root ginger
2 stalks of celery, cut into crescent-shaped pieces
2 spring onions
2 large mangoes, peeled and cut lengthways into strips

Marinade

1 tablesp. light soy sauce
1 tablesp. sherry
1 tablesp. cornflour

To Serve

115 g (4 oz) toasted sliced or slivered almonds
Spring onions

Marinate the chicken strips for at least 2–3 hours but preferably overnight. Drain and add to the hot oil, tossing well for 4–5 minutes. Add the remaining ingredients, then pour on the marinade, which should thicken the mixture slightly. Cook for a further 2–3 minutes, then serve hot with rice, garnished with toasted nuts and spring onions.

Serves 4

Stir-Fry Medley

Here is a really good way to serve cooked vegetables with just that little bit of bite. Stir-frying is a healthy method of cookery if the oil is low in saturated fats and is used sparingly.

An assortment of vegetables: broccoli, cauliflower, mangetout, mushrooms, green and red pepper, onions, cucumber, bean sprouts
285 g (10 oz) peeled prawns

Heat a little oil in a wok, testing the temperature before stir-frying the vegetables, starting with those that require a rather longer cooking time. Cook no longer than five minutes, seasoning and using a little soy sauce for flavouring. Chicken or any fish can be added to turn this dish into a more substantial main course. Serve on a bed of rice.

Buttermilk and Oatmeal Bread

225 g (8 oz) strong white flour
115 g (4 oz) fine oatmeal
115 g (4 oz) coarse wholewheat flour
1 teasp. bicarbonate of soda
2 dessertsp. honey
280 ml (½ pint) approx. buttermilk
Poppy or sunflower seeds for the top

Begin by mixing the flours and bicarbonate of soda thoroughly in a bowl. Add the honey, and use the buttermilk to mix to a soft dough. Knead lightly to get the surface smooth, then either put it in a loaf tin or on a baking sheet. Brush the top with low-fat milk, and sprinkle with poppy or sunflower seeds if wished, and bake at 200 °C (400 °F or regulo 6) for 25 minutes approximately.

If the crust on top of the loaf is becoming very firm and brown, cover it with a sheet of foil. (I like to use buttermilk in bread-making as I feel the crust is softer, and often the bread will keep better—that is, if there is any left.) Wrap the bread in a tea-towel when it comes out of the oven; don't forget to 'tap its bottom' to check if it is well cooked.

Serves 6

Sunny Soda Bread

225 g (8 oz) wholemeal flour
115 g (4 oz) plain flour
55 g (2 oz) oatmeal
2 level teasp. baking soda
Pinch of cream of tartar
55 g (2 oz) sunflower margarine
55 g (2 oz) sunflower seeds
Buttermilk

Sieve the flour, baking soda and cream of tartar into a bowl. Add the wholemeal flour and oatmeal. Cut and rub in the margarine. Add half the sunflower seeds and the buttermilk to mix to a soft dough. Turn onto a floured board, knead lightly, then either shape into a cob or put into a loaf tin. Brush over the top with a little beaten egg or milk, sprinkle with the remaining sunflower seeds, and bake at 220 °C (425 °F or regulo 7) for 20–25 minutes. Don't forget to tap the bottom of the bread: if it sounds hollow it should be ready.

Strawberry Flummery

Fools, flummeries and snows are made from the fruits of the season.

450 g (1 lb) strawberries
280 ml (½ pint) low-fat strawberry yoghurt
15 g (½ oz) gelatine powder in 3 tablesp. water
1 large egg white
1 banana
2 teasp. lemon juice

Sieve the strawberries into a bowl, then chop or mash the banana with the lemon juice. Add the yoghurt to the sieved strawberries and banana, mixing well. Slowly add the prepared gelatine, pouring gently and mixing carefully. Finally add the well-beaten egg white, folding the mixture to hold in the trapped air. Turn into a serving dish and decorate with sieved raspberry purée. Chill in the fridge until set (approximately 1 hour), then serve.

Serves 6–8

Nutty Fruit Crumble

Wholemeal flour and oats are used to boost the fibre value of this crumble topping, and a minimum of sugar is used. Alternatively, a muesli mix could be used instead.

680 g (1½ lb) fruit in season or mixture of fruits: cherries, blackcurrants, apples, blackberries, gooseberries, plums
55 g (2 oz) wholemeal (or half white, half wholemeal) flour
55 g (2 oz) jumbo or porridge oats
1 teasp. mixed spice
55 g (2 oz) margarine
55 g (2 oz) brown sugar (or artificial sweetener)
30 g (1 oz) hazelnuts

Prepare the fruit, and place it in an ovenproof dish. Mix together the flour, oats, and mixed spice, rub in the margarine, stir in the sugar and nuts, then spoon the mixture over the fruit. Bake in a preheated oven at 180 °C (350 °F or regulo 4) for 25–30 minutes until the fruit is tender.

Serve with natural low-fat yoghurt, semi-skimmed milk, or skimmed-milk custard.

Serves 6

9. Making the Most of Mince

We really don't make the most of mince; all too often we use it when we can't think of anything else to cook. I have even heard it referred to as the poor cousin of sirlon steak. But mince is the ultimate convenience food. Children love it, it has been the traditional food of so many countries, and all it needs is just a good pinch of imagination to turn it into something special.

There is a tendency to think of mince only as the raw steak bought from a butcher's or supermarket, but your butcher will willingly mince beef, pork, lamb or bacon for you.

Both coarse and finely ground mince have their use in cooking. Of course burgers hold their shape better during cooking when the meat is finely minced, but if it has been refrigerated it will become firm and is easier to mince. Remember that minced cooked meat requires thorough reheating.

Mince can be cooked in a great variety of ways; grilling and barbecuing are two of the healthiest methods. If you are frying it in a non-stick pan, use the minimum of fat or oil; also try to avoid adding water to mince during the initial cooking. Make sure you don't overcrowd the pan when browning mince, otherwise it will be a poor colour.

Shepherd's pie has always been a popular favourite in many homes. Our not-so-down-to-earth version combines savoy cabbage, shredded parsnip and swede with the mince, and has a simple diced potato topping. This is always popular with my hungry family.

Camus cottage meatloaf has a most unusual texture, is good either hot or cold, and is a wonderful stand-by to have in the freezer.

Nothing could be more simple than my hotchpotch, a dish that turns mince, potatoes, onions and parsley into a filling and satisfying supper.

Farmhouse pie uses a very quick pastry, rather similar to flaky pastry but made with much less effort. It combines minced lamb with seasonal mint and potatoes to create a very versatile pie. Minced pork with sage and one small grated cooking apple gives a very different variation.

The dinner party mince is based on bobotie, a traditional South African recipe. The mango chutney, raisins, sultanas, apples and spices all combine to transform the mince into a rather exotic dish.

Dinner Party Mince

This is a way of livening up your mince to dinner-party status: a most interesting dish of mince lightly flavoured with spices and chutney and cooked with a custardy topping.

450 g (1 lb) minced beef
450 g (1 lb) chopped onions
115 g (4 oz) raisins
115 g dry roasted peanuts
3 tablesp. curry powder
6 tablesp. mango chutney
1 tablesp. lemon juice
Salt and pepper
3 eggs
2 bay leaves
280 ml (½ pint) full-cream milk
(2 oz) breadcrumbs
1 medium cooking apple
1 dessertsp. olive oil

Season the mince well with freshly milled black pepper, and set it aside. Next make the sauce: fry the onion in the oil, add the curry powder, breadcrumbs, nuts, chutney, lemon juice, raisins, apple, and seasoning. Add the minced steak to the sauce, but do not continue to cook at this stage. Using a large bowl mix the mince well into the sauce. Transfer the mixture to a large dish, place the bay leaves on top, cover with foil, and bake at 180 °C (350 °F or regulo 4) for 1 hour.

Discard the bay leaves, beat the eggs with the milk, season with salt and pepper, pour over the meat, and return to the oven uncovered and bake at the same temperature for another 30 minutes until the top has coloured and set.

A Not-So-Down-to-Earth Shepherd's Pie

Most of us probably eat less meat today than we did a few years ago. Now we are using the more traditional recipes but combining them rather cleverly with vegetables to create some very good dishes indeed. This version of shepherd's pie does just this.

450 g (1 lb) lean minced steak
½ level teasp. fresh or dried thyme
2 level tablesp. tomato purée
1 large Spanish onion, finely chopped
1 dessertsp. sunflower oil
30 g (1 oz) flour
¼ savoy cabbage, very finely shredded
1 large parsnip, finely sliced
¼ swede, finely sliced
Salt and pepper
280 ml (½ pint) beef or vegetable stock
4–5 dessertsp. parsley, finely chopped

Topping

680 g (1½ lb) cooked and finely mashed potatoes or boiled diced potatoes with skins on
2 egg yolks
55 g (2 oz) low-fat cheese, finely grated

In a flameproof casserole heat the oil and gently cook the onion for 2–3 minutes. Then turn the heat up, add the beef, and brown it well, stirring it around. Next sprinkle in the flour, stir it in to soak up the juices, and then add the tomato purée. Allow to cook for 10 minutes before the stock is added. Simmer gently until cooked.

Lightly steam the savoy cabbage, parsnip, and swede. These vegetables can either be tossed with the minced steak or layered alternately on top of the mince in an ovenproof dish. Finish off the dish with mashed potatoes, either tossed with a fork or piped. (The addition of egg yolk softens the potato and prevents souring, which often occurs if milk is used and the dish frozen.) Bake at 180 °C (350 °F or regulo 4) for 20–25 minutes.

For a quicker version, diced cooked potatoes can be tossed on top and sprinkled with a little cheese and plenty of freshly chopped parsley.

Uplifted Leeks

This is a very easy-to-make rich supper dish that uses both the tender green part of the leek and the white part. Here I have used pork, finely minced and combined with aromatic fresh root ginger, used here with the most tender of spring onions. The initial cooking of the pork and spices allows the leeks to be served slightly crunchy.

4–6 leeks
340 g (12 oz) minced lean pork
115 g (4 oz) wholemeal breadcrumbs
2–3 spring onions, finely chopped
1 clove of garlic
1 lightly beaten egg
1 dessertsp. olive oil
140 ml (¼ pint) dry white wine
140 ml (¼ pint) vegetable stock

In a bowl mix the raw minced pork with the freshly squeezed ginger juice, clove of garlic, and finely chopped spring onion. Fry in the olive oil for 5–6 minutes, tossing often, then cool.

Prepare the leeks by chopping off the coarse green leaves from the top after splitting some distance along the length of the leek to allow any dirt to escape when gently rinsed in cold water. Allow the leeks to stand in a jug of cold water, upside down; pat them dry, then split them down the centre.

To the pork mixture add the breadcrumbs and beaten egg. Fill the leeks, tie them securely with string, then toss them in hot oil until just coated. Transfer them to an ovenproof dish, pour on the stock and white wine, and braise for 35–40 minutes.

Serves 4–6

Camus Cottage Meatloaf

This is an ideal way of cooking and serving minced steak. The gentle method of baking in the oven combines the flavours of the sausage meat and minced steak well together. This dish is good served either hot or cold, with baked potatoes or pickles and salad.

450 g (1 lb) lean minced beef
170 g (6 oz) pork sausage-meat
1 large onion, finely chopped or grated
1 small green pepper, chopped
2 dessertsp. tomato purée
2 cloves of garlic
85 g (3 oz) white breadcrumbs
85 g (3 oz) grated carrot
2 tablesp. chopped parsley
½ teasp. chopped sage or thyme or mixed herbs
2 large eggs, well beaten
Salt
Freshly milled black pepper
½ teasp. paprika pepper

In a large bowl mix the minced steak, sausage-meat, grated onion and carrot, freshly chopped garlic, pepper, breadcrumbs, parsley, and seasoning. Mix well together, using a wooden spoon (or you may find it easier to bind and mix all the ingredients with your hand). Use the well-beaten egg to bind the ingredients together, then transfer to a 900 g (2 lb) loaf tin. You may line the tin carefully with foil to avoid any discoloration of some tins. Press down well, and bake on the middle shelf of the oven at 190 °C (375 °F or regulo 5) for 1¼–1½ hours, until firm to the touch and leaving the sides of the tin. To avoid shrinkage of this loaf, stand the tin in a roasting pan with enough boiling water to come half way up the sides of the tin.

Leave to cool for 15 minutes, tilt the tin, and pour off the juices. If serving cold, set aside in a cool place overnight to allow the flavours to blend and mature.

Serves 8

Farmhouse Pie

1 onion, chopped
2–3 large potatoes, peeled and chopped
450 g (1 lb) mince (pork or lamb)
2–3 tablesp. chopped herbs (mint for lamb, sage for pork)
Salt
Black pepper
1 dessertsp. oil

Pastry

450 g (1 lb) plain flour
340 g (12 oz) fat, preferably butter
½ teasp. salt
Cold water to mix to a soft dough

To make the pastry, sieve the flour and salt into a bowl, grate in the butter, then chop through with a knife. The pastry will mix better if the fat is put in the freezer for 15 minutes before grating. Use cold water to mix to a soft dough. Cover and allow to relax in the fridge for half an hour before rolling out.

Next make the filling. Lightly cook the minced lamb in a pan with 1 dessertsp. oil, add the seasoning, and then allow to cool. When cold, add the lightly steamed potatoes and chopped herbs.

Roll out two-thirds of the pastry to line a 200–230 mm (8–9 in.) round-bottomed tin. Brush the bottom and sides of the pastry with beaten egg to prevent the juice leaking through the pastry. Pack the pie full with the filling, then use the remaining one-third of the pastry to cover the top. Seal the edges well with water. Garnish with pastry leaves, and bake at 200 °C (400 °F or regulo 6) for 15 minutes, reducing the temperature to 180 °C (350 °F or regulo 5) for a further 15 minutes or until the pie is evenly browned and well cooked.

Serve hot or cold.

Braised Mushroom Dumplings with Red-Hot Spicy Sauce

These dumplings are good served on a bed of buttered noodles, or with a crisp green salad or a hot potato salad.

450 g (1 lb) lean minced beef
225 g (8 oz) very finely chopped mushrooms
¾ teasp. oregano
1 egg
115 g (4 oz) white breadcrumbs
2 tablesp. chopped parsley
1 dessertsp. tomato purée
1 medium onion, minced
Flour to coat the dumplings
Oil to fry

Sauce

450 g (1 lb) ripe tomatoes, peeled and chopped
1 onion
2 cloves of garlic
½ teasp. paprika
½ red pepper
½ green pepper

Make the dumplings first by mixing the minced steak, lightly fried onion and mushrooms, breadcrumbs, parsley, tomato purée, and egg, binding well together. With your hands, shape the mixture into dumplings, using about a tablespoonful at a time. This quantity should make approximately 12–14 dumplings. Coat each one with flour, then brown in hot oil in a frying pan. When well seared, transfer to an ovenproof dish and pour on any of the juices left in the pan.

Prepare the sauce by lightly frying the onion and garlic in a pan; add the red and green peppers and roughly chopped tomatoes, and simmer for a few minutes. Add a little seasoning and stock to adjust the consistency of the sauce. Pour over the dumplings and cook for 1 hour at 190 °C (375 or regulo 5).

Just before serving, remove the lid of the pot and cook for a further 10 minutes. Sprinkle with finely chopped herbs.

Serves 6–7

Hotchpotch

This dish falls into the same category as those childhood favourites, pan haggerty and bubble-and-squeak, all consisting of a combination of meat and potatoes. Leftovers are fine for this rather special hotchpotch.

450 g (1 lb) lean minced steak
2 onions, sliced into rings
1 dessertsp. sunflower oil to fry
2 tablesp. freshly chopped parsley
Salt and freshly ground black pepper
680 g (1½ lb) boiled, evenly sliced potatoes

Brown the onions in the pan with hot oil, add the minced steak, and toss well over a high temperature until well cooked (12–15 minutes). Add the sliced cooked potatoes, and toss lightly in the pan until well heated throughout; a little vegetable stock may be needed to ensure even cooking.

Serve piping hot, garnished with chopped parsley or seasonal herbs. This dish is particularly good with a red-hot bean salad.

Monday Bake

Minced steak and celeriac transform the simple shepherd's pie into a tasty casserole. With its nutty-sweet celery flavour, celeriac is one of the few vegetables where big is beautiful and more tasty. The flesh discolours when sliced, and so must be placed immediately in acidulated water: 570 ml (1 pint) water with 2 teasp. lemon juice.

450 g (1 lb) minced steak or lamb
1 dessertsp. sunflower oil
1 large onion, finely chopped
225 g (3 evenly sliced) potatoes } **lightly steamed**
225 g (8 oz) peeled and diced celeriac } **lightly steamed**

Festive chocolate yule log.

Bramleys at their best.

Ring-a-ring of rosy fruits.

Buttermilk and oatmeal bread.

Cranberry muffins and mulled wine.

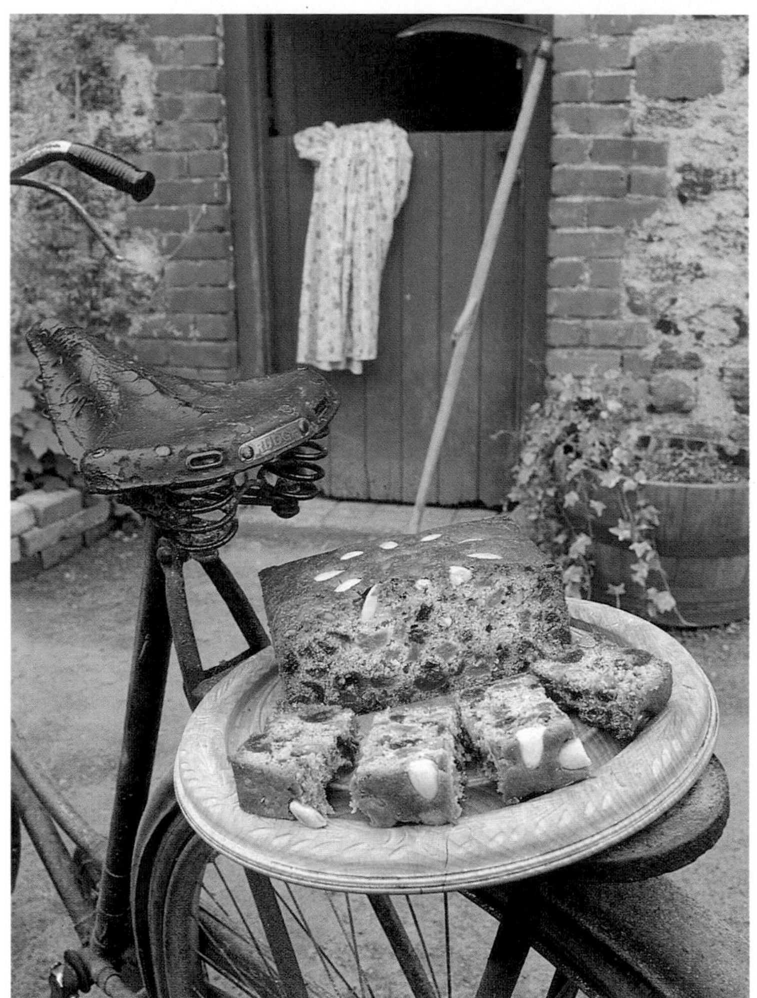

Picnic fruit cake.

Baked rice meringue with drunken raisins.

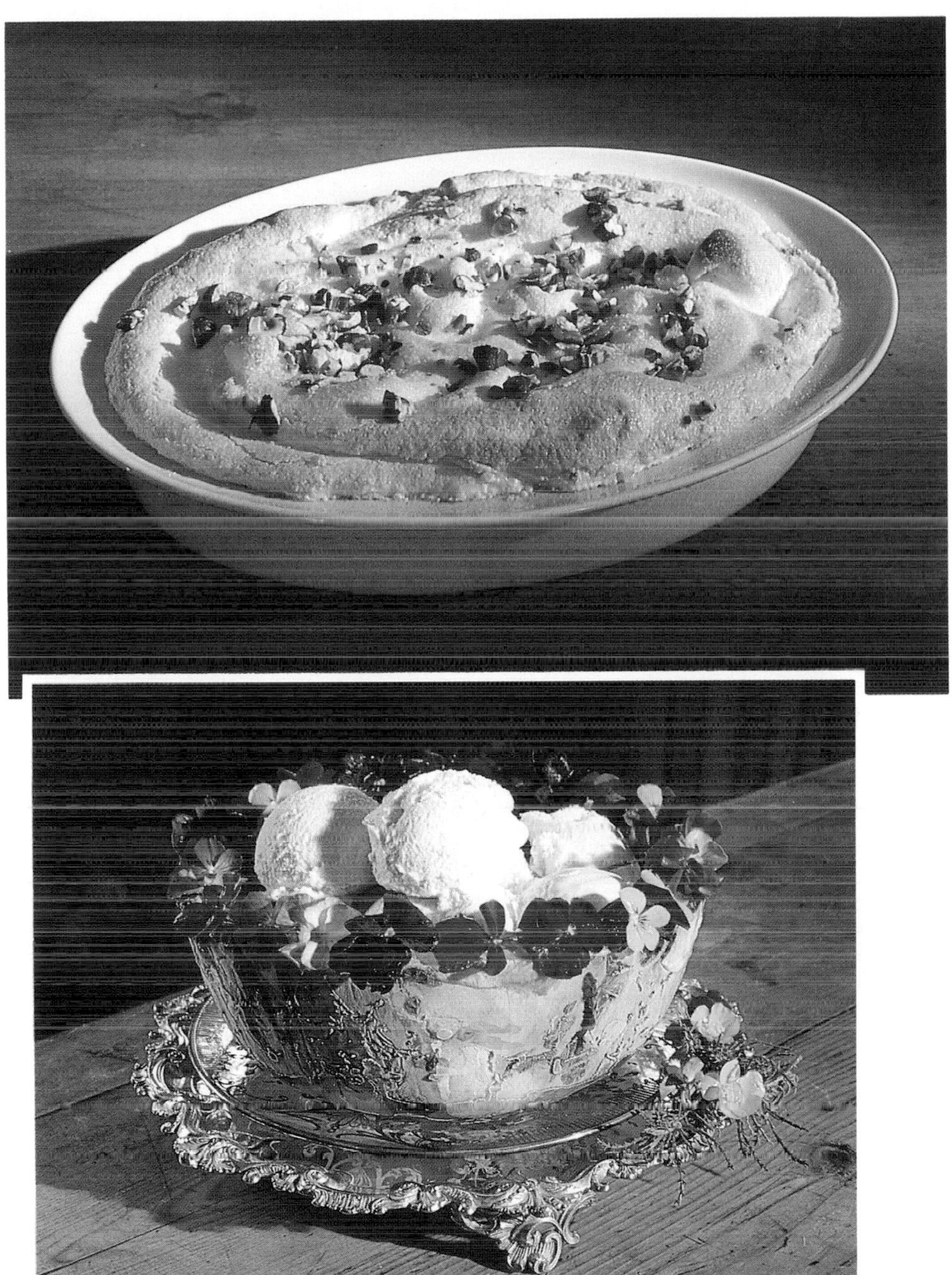

Honey and lavender ice cream in a primrose and violet ice bowl.

Midsummer's dream.

Geranium-leaf sorbet.

Nutty fruit crumble.

Jenny's plum pudding.

Rachel Jane's fairy cakes and chocolate mice.

Jenny with Peter, Jane and Robert.

Topping

1 carton low-fat natural yoghurt
170 g (6 oz) low-fat grated cheese
A pinch of mustard
Salt and black pepper

Lightly toss the finely chopped onion in the hot fat or oil. Add the minced steak, and cook until evenly browned. Transfer to a greased casserole dish. This meaty base can be further livened up by the addition of fresh or tinned tomatoes.

On top of the meat arrange the celeriac and potatoes, which can be lightly steamed for no longer than 10 minutes. A little lemon juice added to the steaming water again helps to keep the vegetables white.

The topping is simply made by mixing the yoghurt and cheese together, then spooning it over the vegetables. Bake at 180 °C (350 °F or regulo 4) for 35–45 minutes or until it is bubbling nicely and golden-brown.

10. Oh, Look Who's Here!

Of course we all like to see our friends and relatives drop in unexpectedly, but so often our enjoyment of their visit can be tinged with anxiety about how to give them something to eat when we haven't got the shopping done or the larder is almost empty. Then of course there may be that other situation when suddenly an important colleague is coming in half an hour's time and a meal to impress is called for. So with these thoughts in mind I have put together some dishes with whatever you happen to have in tins or packets or in the freezer.

The speckled speedy griddle cakes have been aerated with apples and sultanas; this will make sure they cook more quickly, and I can assure you this is one dish you won't even have to serve: they disappear from the griddle as fast as I can make them.

Mother Hubbard's pie is all about going to the cupboard and finding it bare; but even on a very bad day most of us can rustle up bacon, eggs, and cheese, and using these basic ingredients provide a filling dish that is good with a bowl of salad.

Spiced-up ham takes a tin of cooked ham and with the addition of a very hot spicy sauce creates a dish with the minimum of effort and the maximum of impact.

Baked potatoes with a variety of fillings are a good stand-by for the visitors who have different likes and dislikes, especially those with children. The microwave is invaluable here, for baked potatoes cook so quickly. The sausage and bacon bakes are always popular with children, and the crunchy carrot bakes are a good, healthy filling for someone watching the calories. The ham bakes are a substantial filling lightly flavoured with curried chutney.

Dromona chicken is one of our firm family favourites and can so easily be adapted to use either fresh, frozen or tinned chicken, with a tasty sauce using a tinned soup as the basis, and toppings from sliced potatoes to crushed potato crisps, cheese, and wholemeal crumbs. This dish bakes in the oven, requires little attention, and always looks good.

For that impromptu dinner party or for that special guest whom you really have to impress, try symphony of seafood with champagne sauce—but only if you have a well-stocked freezer. This is just the dish: so good with pasta, and an invaluable food to have in your food cupboard.

The crustless quiche can be made just as quickly as you would defrost a pie from your freezer. Various fillings can be used, but for me the attraction lies in the fact that there is no making and rolling out of pastry, a time-consuming and messy exercise, especially if your visitors seat themselves in your kitchen and watch you at work, which is what usually happens in our house!

Mother Hubbard's Pie

Here is a dish made by combining ingredients that the most basic of food cupboards should have, even on a bad day.

30 g (1 oz) butter or margarine
1 tablesp. vegetable oil
450 g (1 lb) potatoes (peeled, grated, rinsed, and dried, or cooked potato)
1 onion or leek, chopped
115 g (4 oz) back bacon, chopped
Salt and black pepper
4 eggs (size 3), beaten
1 tablesp. parsley, chopped
2 tomatoes, thinly sliced
85 g (3 oz) cheddar cheese, grated
A few sprigs of parsley

Heat the butter and oil in a large frying pan. Fry the potato, onion and bacon for about 5 minutes, stirring frequently until the onion is soft. Season. Level the mixture in the pan, then slowly pour the beaten eggs. Sprinkle with chopped parsley and cook over a moderate heat until the base is lightly browned. Neatly arrange the tomato slices on top and sprinkle with cheese; place under a hot grill until the top is set and bubbling; garnish, cut into wedges, and serve hot. Good with a tossed green salad.

Dromona Chicken

This is one of our firm family favourites, a real stand-by recipe that can be changed easily depending on the state of the cupboard. I prefer to make it with fresh chicken pieces and lightly boiled potatoes, but tinned chicken pieces are fine if you adjust the seasoning to bring out the flavours.

285 g (10 oz) can of condensed chicken soup
6 tablesp. mayonnaise
200 ml (7 fl. oz) milk
Salt and pepper
450 g (1 lb) fresh or frozen broccoli, cooked and finely chopped into florets
340 g (12 oz) chicken, cooked and diced (tinned or fresh)
450 g (1 lb) potatoes, peeled, sliced, and parboiled
170 g (6 oz) cheese, grated
Chopped parsley to garnish

Mix the soup, mayonnaise, milk and seasoning together. Pour half the soup mixture into a shallow casserole dish. Arrange the broccoli evenly over the soup, then add the chicken and finally the sliced potatoes Pour the remaining soup mixture over the potatoes, and cook for 30 minutes at 200 °C (400 °F or regulo 6). Sprinkle the cheese on top and cook for a further 15 minutes. Garnish and serve.

The potatoes in this dish can be omitted and a crumbly, crunchy topping used instead, by combining a packet of potato crisps with the cheese and 50 g pinhead oatmeal or wholemeal crumbs.

Serves 6

Spiced-Up Ham

For extra speed a packet of mixed creole spices could be used, but I like to vary the flavours in this dish each time I make it. Precooked frozen rice is an excellent stand-by to have in the freezer for that meal required in extra-quick time.

400 g (14 oz) tin of cooked ham
1 tablesp. oil
1 clove of garlic, crushed
1 onion, sliced
25 mm (1 in.) piece of root ginger, peeled and finely chopped, or ground ginger
1 teasp. turmeric
1 teasp. ground cumin
1 teasp. paprika
1 tablesp. flour
140 ml (¼ pint) vegetable stock
400g (14 oz) tin of tomatoes
225 g (8 oz) tin of pineapple cubes in natural juice
1 bay leaf
Salt and pepper
225 g (8 oz) brown or white rice

Heat the oil in a large pan, then cook the garlic, onion and ginger until the onion is soft. Stir in the spices and flour, and cook for about 1 minute. Gradually stir in the stock, tomatoes and pineapple together with the juice. Bring to the boil, add the bay leaf and seasoning, and simmer uncovered for about 10 minutes. Add the ham, simmer for a further 7–10 minutes, and remove the bay leaf.

Serve with rice and a crisp salad.

Serves 4–6

Speckled Speedy Griddle Cakes

These are one of the great delights at tea-time. They are easy to make on a flat iron griddle, which will cook the cakes on top heat, but a heavy frying pan will do if you haven't got a griddle. Good served with a pot of home-made elderflower and lemon curd, or wild strawberry jam.

340 g (12 oz) flour
½ teasp. salt
½ teasp. baking soda
170 g (6 oz) butter or margarine
85 g (3 oz) caster sugar
85 g (3 oz) sultanas
1 small cooking apple, finely chopped
Pinch of cinnamon (optional)
A little buttermilk to mix

Sieve the flour, salt and baking soda into a bowl. Cut and rub in the fat. Add the sugar, sultanas, and chopped apple, and mix to a stiff dough with the buttermilk. Roll out 10–20 mm (⅜–¾ in.) thick on a well-floured board, and cut with a plain cutter. Have the griddle preheated, but do not let it overheat. If the pan is not well seasoned or if you are using a non-stick pan, cover it with a little butter or vegetable oil.

Bake the cakes on the griddle, turning them once until well risen and lightly browned (about 5 minutes each side).

Serve hot or cold with a good pot of hot tea.

Serves 12

Crustless Quiche

A very easy and quick dish that does not involve the making and rolling of pastry. A variety of fillings can be used; here I have used tinned salmon with frozen broccoli.

170 g (6 oz) self-raising flour
55 g (2 oz) bran
6 eggs
¼ teasp. salt
85 g (3 oz) unsaturated margarine
425 ml (¾ pint) milk
1 large onion, finely chopped
115 g (4 oz) mushrooms
1 tin of salmon
225 g (8 oz) broccoli, frozen
Sprinkling of dill and freshly milled black pepper
Grated cheese to flavour and garnish

Sieve the flour and salt into a large bowl, then rub in the margarine, and add the bran. Whisk the eggs, milk, and cheese, mixing well, and add along with the salmon and broccoli. The onion and mushrooms can be slightly cooked in the microwave before also adding at this stage.

Thoroughly grease a quiche dish, then, mixing well, pour the mixture into the dish and bake in the middle shelf of a preheated oven at 180 °C (350 °F or regulo 4) for 30 minutes, until golden-brown and well risen.

Cut and serve hot or cold with wedges of lemon. Good with a tomato and basil salad.

Serves 8

Bread and Onion Pudding

A very economical dish to make, using a few onions, some bread, milk, and eggs. Makes an ideal snack.

12 slices of bread
2 onions, diced
A few caraway seeds
Freshly ground black pepper
425 ml (¾ pint) milk
3 eggs
Dash of Tabasco sauce
6 rashers of bacon, finely chopped
Grated cheese

Trim the crusts from the bread, butter the slices, and cut them into quarters. Place in an ovenproof dish. Sauté the diced onion along with the bacon until golden-brown. Spread half the bacon and onion over the sliced bread and the caraway seeds (caraway greatly assists the digestion). Pour on the remainder of the onion mixture. Add the whisked egg, milk, and Tabasco, pouring carefully over the bread. Sprinkle with cheese and bake at 180 °C (350 °F or regulo 4) for 35–45 minutes. Serve hot.

Rushing Risotto

Salads have an interesting dimension if served hot, and this risotto salad offers a main course or an ideal accompaniment for hot spicy chops.

225 g (8 oz) brown or white rice
280 ml (½ pint) chicken stock
Salt and pepper
115 g (4 oz) fresh garden peas
115 g (4 oz) sweet corn
225 g (8 oz) cubed cooked ham
½ red pepper
½ green pepper
A few spring onions, finely chopped
1 onion
115 g (4 oz) sliced mushrooms

Precook the rice in the chicken stock. Boil rapidly until tender (approximately 10–12 minutes). The chicken stock gives this salad a particularly good flavour.

In a shallow pan lightly fry the onion and mushrooms, add the cubed ham and peppers, and toss gently for a few minutes. In a large bowl mix the cooked hot rice, onion, mushrooms, peppers, cooked ham or bacon pieces, peas, sweet corn, spring onions, or any other vegetables of your choice, such as green beans or broccoli. Toss in a good french dressing, sprinkle with freshly chopped parsley, and serve hot.

Serves 4–6

Baked Potatoes and Suggested Fillings

Choosing and Cooking Potatoes

Choose even-sized, medium to large potatoes—ideal weight 225 g (8 oz). Prick the potatoes with a fork, place on a baking tray, and bake at 220 °C

(425 °F or regulo 7) for 1–1½ hours. When cooked, make a crosswise incision on top using a sharp knife, and squeeze the potato gently in a cloth until the cross opens at all four points.

To cook jacket potatoes in the microwave oven, pierce the potato with a fork, then place it on a double thickness of absorbent kitchen paper in the microwave. Each potato will take about 6–8 minutes to cook. The result of cooking by this method is that the potatoes do not bake—i.e. they will not have a crisp skin. Ideally you should half-cook the potatoes in the microwave and then transfer them to the oven to crispen.

Sausage and Bean Bakes

4 potatoes, scrubbed and baked
225 g (8 oz) sausages
450 g (1 lb) tin of baked beans
1 teasp. mixed herbs
Salt and black pepper
Parsley to garnish

Grill the sausages, then cut them into quarters. Place the baked beans in a saucepan with the sausages, mixed herbs, and seasoning, and simmer for 5 minutes, stirring occasionally. Make a crosswise incision in the potatoes, and open them out by pressing at the base. Divide the filling between the potatoes, and serve garnished with parsley.

Serves 4

Crunchy Carrot Bakes

4 potatoes, scrubbed and baked
1 green apple
1 tablesp. lemon juice
170 g (6 oz) carrots, grated
115 g (4 oz) cheese, grated
55 g (2 oz) hazelnuts, chopped
55 g (2 oz) sultanas
Salt and black pepper
Parsley to garnish

Dice the apple and sprinkle with lemon juice. Place the carrot and cheese in a bowl. Add the apple, hazelnuts and sultanas, season, and mix well. Make a crosswise incision in the potatoes and open out by pressing out at the base. Divide the filling between the potatoes and serve garnished with parsley.

Serves 4

Ham Bakes

A quick filling for baked potatoes.

4 potatoes, scrubbed
170 g (6 oz) back bacon, rinded and chopped
55 g (2 oz) mushrooms, sliced
30 g (1 oz) butter
2 tablesp. curried chutney
Salt and pepper
Chopped parsley to garnish

Place the potatoes in the microwave and cook for 15 minutes. Meanwhile place all the remaining ingredients into a small glass bowl and mix well. Put the bowl in the microwave with the potatoes and cook for 2 minutes. Stir well and cook for a further 2 minutes, until the potato-and-bacon mixture is cooked. Make a crosswise incision in the top of each potato and divide the filling between each, adding extra butter to the potato if needed. Garnish with chopped parsley and serve.

Symphony of Seafood in Champagne Sauce

Here is a dish that comes together in minutes, but only if you have a well-stocked freezer. This light and delicate sauce combines extremely well with a variety of seafood.

680–900 g (1½–2 lb) assorted seafood: salmon, prawns, scallops, smoked trout, lemon sole, or turbot

Sauce

55 g (2 oz) butter
140 ml (¼ pint) fish stock
140 ml (¼ pint) dry champagne or dry white sparkling wine
12 g (½ oz) cornflour
280 ml (½ pint) whipping cream
115 g (4 oz) finely sliced leeks
A pinch of cayenne and black pepper
225 g (8 oz) pasta

Cook the pasta in boiling water to which 1–2 teasp. olive oil has been added. (This prevents the pasta sticking together during cooking.)

Melt the butter in a large pan and lightly toss the defrosted uncooked fish for 1–2 minutes. After cooking remove from the pan and cook the sauce. To the melted butter add the fish stock and finely sliced leeks and cook rapidly for a further 2 minutes. Add the champagne, lightly whipped cream and blended cornflour and cook until bubbling lightly. Do not overcook or the sauce will become thin. Return all the fish to the pan, stirring very gently until all the fish is lightly cooked (2–3 minutes).

Adjust the seasoning, and serve on a bed of lightly buttered pasta.

In this dish the flavour will be improved if it is made with a good fish stock. Remember it can be made very easily and frozen, then used on demand.

Fish Stock

Bones of 2–3 filleted fish
1 onion, roughly sliced
1 carrot
1 leek
570 ml (1 pint) water
Salt, a few peppercorns, a small bunch of parsley

Place all the ingredients in a pan, bring slowly to the boil, and simmer gently for 30 minutes. Strain to remove any scum, then cool before freezing.

11. Meatless Menus

With the growing trend towards meatless cooking, especially among the younger generation, one of the main concerns for any cook must be to provide the family with meals that are nutritionally well balanced. Today, with the shelves in our supermarkets, local stores and health shops so well stocked with endless varieties of pasta, rice, lentils, nuts, beans and soya products, with herbs, spices, and grains and of course fresh fruits and vegetables available all the year round, it is not a problem to provide well-balanced and interesting meatless menus that are not just snacks but real, wholesome meals.

The meatless moussaka is a very colourful and substantial dish made with a variety of ingredients, such as pulses, containing plenty of protein, and soya milk, nutritionally very good, with vitamin B_{12}, one of the nutrients most likely to be missing in this type of diet. Tofu is also an invaluable ingredient, as it combines so well to create good sauces.

The three-bean salad, served either hot or cold, makes an ideal main course with a good crusty bread.

Stir frying is a most useful way of cooking. Usually 3 to 4 minutes is enough to cook most vegetables, and this method gives a very distinctive flavour. Use one of the healthier vegetable oils, such as virgin olive oil or sunflower oil. Crispy noodles can also be stir-fried, giving a very crunchy accompaniment to stir-fried fresh garden vegetables.

The vegetarian burgers are always popular at a barbecue; don't worry, they won't fall apart. The secret is to chop the nuts and all the ingredients very finely and bind well with two lightly beaten eggs. I find it a good idea when they are shaped into little rounds to allow them at least 30 minutes in the refrigerator to firm up.

I find Paddy's cake an alternative to serving rice. This rice cake cuts out nicely and can be served either hot or cold with casseroles.

Cakes packed with fruit are great favourites of mine. I created the windfall cake to use the abundance of pears, apples and plums that occasionally get ahead of me. In this cake the fruit can be varied. I love its lack of uniformity, and believe me, it does taste good. Occasionally I serve it dusted with icing sugar and a little fromage frais.

Mushroom Risotto

The colour, flavour and appearance of this dish can be greatly changed by the quality of rice used and the type of mushroom. If you are using wild rice, cook it a little longer; but it freezes well, so larger quantities can be cooked at one time.

225 g (8 oz) mushrooms
225 (8 oz) risotto rice or 170 g (6 oz) plain rice and 55 g (2 oz) wild rice
1 small onion
1 carrot, coarsely grated
425 ml (¾ pint) vegetable stock
140 ml (¼ pint) dry white wine
Salt and pepper

Melt the fat in a pan, or, if using oil, simply heat and add the onion and cook for 5 minutes. Add the finely sliced mushrooms and grated carrots and cook for 2–3 minutes. Add the partly cooked rice, vegetable stock, white wine, and seasoning, and allow the risotto to simmer gently until the stock has been absorbed.

Garnish with chopped parsley and a few sliced cooked mushrooms. Serve with mangetout peas, lightly buttered.

Vegetarian Burgers

Eating outdoors has become more popular, and these vegetarian burgers are ideal for the barbecue.

115 g (4 oz) finely chopped onion
30 g (1 oz) margarine
115 g (4 oz) mixed nuts
115 g (4 oz) unsalted peanuts
115 g (4 oz) wholemeal breadcrumbs
2 eggs
115 g (4 oz) grated cheese
½ level teasp. sage
Black pepper

Fry the onion lightly in the melted margarine. Add all the other ingredients, and shape into rounds; these can either be cooked in a pan or cooked on the barbecue.

Makes 8–10 burgers

Three-Bean Salad

This dish needs no accompaniment except good bread, and can be served either hot or cold.

225 g (8 oz) runner beans
225 g (8 oz) french beans
225 g (8 oz) broad beans
170 g (6 oz) brown rice
Rind and juice of one large orange
55 g (2 oz) sunflower seeds, hazelnuts, walnuts
4 peaches } cut into thin slices
4 nectarines }
140 ml (¼ pint) yoghurt
Herbs: lemon thyme, rosemary, garlic

Cook the rice with the juice and rind of an orange. Cook the beans by steaming, allowing a slightly shorter time for the french beans (3–5 minutes). Combine the rice with the beans, toasted nuts, peaches and nectarines. Use the yoghurt to mix the entire salad well together. Season well and add a few herbs to help develop the flavour: lemon thyme, rosemary, and garlic.

Serve hot or cold, garnished with crescent shapes of nectarines and peaches.

Serves 10–12

Courgette Casserole

This is an excellent recipe for using larger courgettes that are too big to use as a cooked vegetable dish. I often salt sliced courgettes before cooking to extract some of their water.

3 courgettes, diced
1 red pepper
1 green pepper
2–3 chillies
1 large onion
1 clove of garlic
2 teasp. curry powder
1 teasp. cumin powder
1 teasp. lemon juice
400 g (14 oz) tin of tomatoes
140 ml (¼ pint) chicken or vegetable stock
1 dessertsp. cooking oil
225 g (8 oz) diced potatoes

In a bowl mix together the curry powder, and cumin. Put the onion and garlic in a medium-sized casserole and fry gently in the oil for 2–3 minutes. Add the sliced courgettes, peppers, and chillies. Cover, and cook for a further 4 minutes. Add the tomatoes, potatoes, seasoning, and stock. Cover, and cook for 5–8 minutes.

This can be served with wholemeal breadcrumbs and grated cheese on top, or simply with a swirl of natural yoghurt.

Serves 6

Stir-Fried Garden-Fresh Vegetables and Buttered Noodles

4 tablesp. clear honey
4 tablesp. light soy sauce
1 tablesp. sherry or vinegar
Freshly ground black pepper
1 tablesp. vegetable oil, olive oil, or groundnut oil
1 teasp. fresh ginger, peeled
2 cloves of garlic, finely grated
1 red pepper } seeded and cut into thin strips
1 green pepper }
1 carrot, peeled and cut into thin strips
115 g (4 oz) mushrooms
170 g (6 oz) snow peas
8–10 shallots
200 g (7 oz) broccoli, broken into small florets and blanched
140 ml (¼ pint) vegetable stock

Mix together the honey, soy sauce, and sherry or vinegar; season well. Add the carrot, pepper, mushrooms, and all the coloured vegetables (not the green ones). Heat the oil in a large wok or frying pan and fry the garlic and ginger. Toss around, then add the drained coloured vegetables. Stir gently to coat all the vegetables with oil, and cook for 1 minute. Add the remaining vegetables and toss together lightly, pour on the remainder of the marinade and cook for 2 minutes. The marinade can be blended with 15 g (½ oz) cornflour or arrowroot if a slightly thicker sauce is preferred.

Serve piping hot, garnished with sliced shallots and toasted almonds. Good to serve with rice or noodles.

Serves 6

Gratifying Spinach and Salmon

This is one of my favourite snack and starter dishes, which combines assorted vegetables in a very tasty sauce. If the budget will not stretch to smoked salmon it can easily be omitted.

170 g (6 oz) spinach
115 g (4 oz) smoked salmon
55 g (2 oz) spring onions
2–3 finely sliced potatoes
Oil for brushing
Black pepper and lemon juice

Sauce

140 ml (¼ pint) soured cream
570 ml (1 pint) soya milk
115 g (4 oz) mozarella cheese
2 level tablesp. grated parmesan cheese
30 g (1 oz) white flour
30 g (1 oz) butter
2 egg yolks and 2 egg whites

Wash the spinach and remove any of the tough stalks. Cook gently in water for 5 minutes until well softened. Squeeze out excess moisture and chop finely. Lightly boil the finely sliced potatoes and arrange in the bottom of lightly greased gratin dishes. Layer with the lightly cooked spinach and smoked salmon, sprinkled with a little lemon juice and black pepper. Pour on half the soured cream.

Make the sauce next by melting the butter in a small pan, stir in the flour, and cook, stirring for 1 minute until thickened. Remove from the heat, whisk in the egg yolks, soured cream, and half the mozarella cheese, and mix well. Finally fold in the whisked egg whites and pour the sauce over the gratin dishes. Sprinkle with mozarella and parmesan cheese, and bake at 200 °C (400 °F or regulo 6) until golden-brown (about 10 minutes).

These little souffléd gratins will hold well, and can be served with a mixed salad and little new potatoes.

Serves 6

Meatless Moussaka

2 medium aubergines, cut into rounds
2 medium onions
2 cloves of garlic
1 green pepper
4 sliced potatoes
170 g (6 oz) brown or green lentils
115 g (4 oz) split peas, green or yellow
570 ml (1 pint) hot water
2 celery stalks
2 dessertsp. tomato purée
4 large tomatoes, skinned
1 dessertsp. finely chopped parsley
Olive oil

Topping

55 g (2 oz) fat **55 g (2 oz) plain flour** **570 ml (1 pint) soya milk** **55 g (2 oz) cheddar cheese**	**or 225 g (8 oz) tofu** **and** **55 g (2 oz) vegetarian cheese**

2 eggs
A little nutmeg or mace

Wash the lentils and split peas and simmer in 570 ml (1 pint) of water for approximately 1 hour. Cut the potatoes into slices and lightly boil for 5 minutes with a teasp. of lemon juice. Slice the aubergine, and sprinkle with a little salt and lemon juice. Press down to remove a little of the excess moisture in the aubergines: the salt will help to extract it.

In a pan fry the onion, garlic, and pepper; after 5 minutes add the celery, cooked lentil mixture, tomatoes, tomato purée, and seasoning. Leave to simmer for 15 minutes.

Prepare the aubergines by frying lightly in a pan until lightly browned, then cover the base of the dish with half the quantity. Layer the cooked vegetable mixture on top, finishing with a layer of aubergines, then sliced potatoes. Finish by pouring the sauce over the top and sprinkling with cheese, and bake at 180 °C (350 °F or regulo 4) until brown and golden on top.

This is a typical white sauce, made by the roux method, with the addition of lightly whisked eggs as the sauce is cooling. Adjust the seasoning to taste.

Silken tofu, mixed with a little cheese, can be used instead of the white sauce. Spice it up with plenty of seasoning, such as paprika or cayenne pepper.

Serves 6

Leeks and Onions in a Hot Mustardy Sauce

This is an easy, economical and satisfying dish, suitable for a supper or as a vegetable accompaniment. For minimum wastage and tender eating choose leeks with long, thin white stems: stout white parts are nearly always tough, and the coarse greenery of leeks is never pleasant to eat.

30 g (1 oz) fat or unsaturated oil
2–3 leeks
2 onions

Sauce
280 ml (½ pint) low-fat milk
30 g (1 oz) plain flour
30 g (1 oz) unsaturated fat or butter
Salt and pepper
1 teasp. wholegrain mustard
225 g (8 oz) mashed potatoes for piping

Melt the fat in a large pan, add the thinly sliced leeks and chopped onion. Turn until each piece is lightly coated, then allow to cook for 2–3 minutes. Transfer to a serving dish.

Make the mustardy sauce by the roux method: melt the fat, add the flour, mixing well (off the heat), then gradually blend in the milk, stirring or whisking well. Bring to boiling point and cook for 1 minute until all the starch grains have burst. Add the mustard, then pour over the leeks. Garnish the dish by piping potatoes around the outside. Sprinkle grated cheese over the hot gratin. Cook under a hot grill for a few minutes so that the cheese melts and the potatoes become well toasted.

Serve with plenty of good wholemeal bread to mop up the sauce.

Serves 6

Soup in Pumpkin

1 pumpkin, 4 kg (9 lb)
285 g (10 oz) Gruyère cheese, diced
2–3 cups small croutons
1.1 L (2 pints) cream
Salt, pepper, nutmeg

Choose a well-shaped pumpkin. Cut a bit out of the stem end about 130 mm (5 in.) from the end. Remove seeds and fibres. Put in alternate layers of croutons and cheese to fill three-quarters of the pumpkin. Season with salt, pepper, and nutmeg, then pour the cream into the pumpkin until it is full. Replace the lid (with tinfoil under it), and put the pumpkin in an ovenproof dish with a small rim in case of leakage. Cook at 150 °C (300 °F or regulo 2) for about 3 hours. Every half hour stir the soup gently to make sure it all becomes creamy.

Serve with a large spoon or ladle, giving each person some soup and pumpkin scooped from inside.

Serves 8–10

Cauliflower with a Garlicky Tomato Sauce

Cauliflower can be boiled or steamed whole. However, if it is first separated into individual florets (or curds) it will cook both faster and more evenly. This dish makes a pleasing change from cauliflower au gratin.

1 cauliflower (in florets)
115 g (4 oz) wholemeal breadcrumbs
115 g (4 oz) parmesan cheese
1 can of tomatoes (drained)
3 cloves of garlic
Salt and pepper

Steam the florets for 5–7 minutes (no longer: I feel cauliflower is one vegetable that should be served with a bite). Arrange the drained cauliflower in an ovenproof dish and make the sauce.

Mix the drained tomatoes with 3 cloves of garlic, breadcrumbs, and parmesan cheese, and mix well. Spoon over the cauliflower, and grill or bake for approximately 5 minutes until the cheese begins to melt.

Bittersweet Celery

I find celery rather dull and tasteless, especially when braised, as it loses its bite; but this bittersweet sauce combines beautifully with celery to change this vegetable both in appearance and flavour.

4–5 stalks celery
1 cooking apple, sliced
1 onion, chopped
Small can of pineapple chunks or slices
2 dessertsp. cider vinegar
140 ml (¼ pint) pineapple juice (from drained can)
Salt and pepper
30 g (1 oz) cornflour, blended with 2 tablesp. cold water
1 red or green apple
Celery leaves to garnish
1 dessertsp. cooking oil

Lightly fry the onion and celery together in the hot fat or oil. Add the cooking apple and cook for a further 1–2 minutes. Remove from the heat, and make the sauce. Blend the cornflour with cold water, add to the pineapple juice and cider vinegar, and bring to boiling point, stirring continuously.

A little soy sauce may be added along with the seasoning, perhaps using a little more cider vinegar if a really piquant flavour is preferred. Add the diced pineapple pieces, and pour over the lightly fried celery mixture. Bake at 200 °C (400 °F or regulo 6) for 15–20 minutes.

Serve garnished with wedges of apple and celery leaves. This is good with grilled pork chops.

Serves 6–8

Paddy's Cake

170 g (6 oz) medium-grain rice
½ teasp. salt
½ small Spanish onion, finely chopped
55 g (2 oz) soft butter
55 g (2 oz) self-raising flour
2 tablesp. parsley
1 egg
140 ml (¼ pint) milk
Dash of Worcester sauce
Black pepper
Cheddar cheese

Cook the rice by boiling it in a pan with a pinch of salt and sufficient cold water to cover it. Boil rapidly until the rice is tender; remove from the heat and fluff with a fork. Allow to cool slightly. Combine the softened butter, cheese, onion, parsley, egg, milk, flour, water, sauce, and black pepper; mix well. Finally add the rice, and mix well. Transfer to a 450 g (1 lb) loaf tin, or shape into individual cakes. The cakes can be baked with a cube of cheese lightly pressed on top of each. Bake at 180 °C (250 °F or regulo 4) for 30–35 minutes.

Windfall Cake

This is one of my favourite cakes, created to use up surplus windfall apples, pears, or victoria plums.

340 g (12 oz) prepared apples, pears, or victoria plums
1 teasp. cinnamon
55 g (2 oz) sultanas
55 g (2 oz) ground almonds
115 g (4 oz) sunflower margarine
55 g (2 oz) soft brown sugar
1 tablesp. pear/apple and walnut spread
2 eggs
115 g (4 oz) self-raising flour
1 dessertsp. concentrated apple juice
10–12 whole almonds to decorate
Caster sugar to dredge

Mix the finely chopped apples, sultanas, cinnamon and apple juice together in a bowl. Cream the fat with the sugar, pear and walnut spread. Beat in the egg alternately with the flour and ground almonds. Grease a 180–200 mm (7–8 in.) cake tin, and spread two-thirds of the cake mixture into the bottom of the tin. Cover with the fruit filling, spread the remainder of the cake mixture on top, and decorate with whole almonds. Bake at 180 °C (350 °F or regulo 4) for 45–50 minutes. This can be served either hot or cold.

Serves 8

12. A Passion for Puddings

I once read that to arrive at pudding time is to arrive at the best part of the meal, and I certainly agree with that sentiment. Puddings, desserts, sweets—call them what you will—be they boiled, steamed, or baked, will always be to me honest, down-to-earth ideas flavoured not only with sauces but a little nostalgia.

There are few people today with enough will power, no matter how carefully they count the calories, to resist a shimmering summer fruit ring garlanded with fruits of the forest.

Making your own ice cream is really very easy. All too often people don't try, simply because they feel an ice cream machine is essential for achieving a smooth texture. I feel that if a recipe includes cream and milk, as opposed to a high percentage of water, your ice cream will freeze more successfully in your home freezer. It is good to freeze your ice cream as quickly as possible, and make sure all utensils are cold before starting. The honey and lavender ice cream has a most delicate flavour, reminiscent of the warm summer days in the garden.

How about turning a simple rice pudding into a baked rice meringue with drunken raisins?

King of puddings was always one of the favourite puddings in our home: a very light lemony pudding layered with jam, which can be topped with a crunchy meringue.

Bramleys at their Best is a pudding I have created just for me. Lemons again, but this time in a pastry flavoured with cinnamon and with a filling of apples, apricots, sultanas, nutmeg, and honey.

Never skimp on good-quality ingredients when it comes to the pudding; don't feel one bit guilty, just enjoy them. After all, that's what they are for.

Midsummer's Dream

This is a smooth-flavoured custard enriched with cream and set in a mould: a very delicate pudding, but care must be taken not to be too heavy-handed with the gelatine.

850 ml (1½ pints) milk
6 egg yolks
115 g (4 oz) caster sugar
280 ml (½ pint) cream
4 level. teasp. gelatine
4 dessertsp. warm water
1 vanilla pod
1 cinnamon stick

For the Fruit Salad

450 g (1 lb) assorted seasonal fruits
55 g (2 oz) caster sugar
Rind and juice of 1 orange and 1 lemon

Infuse the cinnamon stick and vanilla pod in the milk. Heat almost to boiling point, then cover, and allow to cool for 15–20 minutes. Beat the egg yolks with the caster sugar until thick and creamy, and pour over the strained, slightly warmed milk. Return to the heat and very slowly stir the mixture until it shows signs of thickening. Pour the custard into a bowl, and set aside to cool (this can be speeded up by placing over a bowl of ice).

Dissolve the gelatine in 4 tablesp. water over a pan of simmering water. Do not allow the gelatine to become too warm or it will lose its setting qualities. Add to the custard, and when beginning to show signs of thickening, fold in the lightly whipped cream. (Mixing is easier if the cream is the same consistency as the thickening custard.) Pour into the lightly greased mould, and chill in the fridge for at least 5 hours. The pudding can be frozen at this stage if required, although if frozen and defrosted it will be slightly softer on thawing.

Mix all the prepared fruits in a bowl, pour on the rind and juice of the orange and lemon, sprinkle with caster sugar, and leave to marinate for 1–2 hours. Serve around the pudding or in a separate dish.

Serves 8

Baked Rice Meringue with Drunken Raisins

A good rice pudding needs time to cook slowly. Be generous in this recipe: plenty of creamy milk, and a good knob of butter. Carolina rice is best.

1.1 L (2 pints) milk
115 g (4 oz) Carolina rice
55 g (2 oz) granulated sugar
55 g (2 oz) butter
A little grated nutmeg
225 g (8 oz) muscatel raisins
140 ml (¼ pint) brandy
Grated rind of 1 lemon

For the Meringue

3 egg whites
Pinch of salt
170 g (6 oz) caster sugar
30 g (1 oz) demerara sugar

Prepare the raisins or sultanas first. Place in a bowl with the lemon rind, grated nutmeg, and brandy. Cover, and leave aside to allow the raisins to absorb the brandy. Next butter a pie dish well and pour in the rice and sugar. Cover with the milk, add the knob of butter, and place on the middle shelf of the oven and bake for 1 hour at 180 °C (350 °F or regulo 4). Stir occasionally. Pour on the drunken raisins, nutmeg, and lemon rind, and stir well into the rice.

Next prepare the meringue. Whisk the egg whites with half the caster sugar until stiff, then gently fold in the remainder of the sugar. Spoon over the top of the rice pudding, and bake in the middle shelf of the oven for a further 20–25 minutes at 150 °C (300 °F or regulo 3) until light golden-brown and firm to the touch.

Sprinkle over with demerara sugar and serve.

Honey and Lavender Ice Cream

Home-made ice cream is well worth the effort. Use this pudding with plenty of imagination, as there are so many flavours and sauces to give ice cream an individuality and character all its own. Some of my favourite flavours are mango and passionfruit, or—especially for the children—a good vanilla ice cream served with hot banana sauce or wild strawberry.

2–3 tablesp. boiling water
2 tablesp. fresh or dried lavender flowers or leaves
3 tablesp. runny honey
4 egg yolks
570 ml (1 pint) milk
30 g (1 oz) caster sugar
1 drop of vanilla essence
570 ml (1 pint) double cream, lightly whipped

Start by making the light egg custard. Beat the eggs and sugar together without making them frothy. Heat the milk until nearly boiling, and pour it gently over the eggs, stirring with a whisk at the same time. Flavour with vanilla, and heat gently over low heat until just showing signs of thickening. Leave to cool.

Make an infusion of the fresh lavender in 2 tablespoonfuls of boiling water; if fresh lavender is not available use dried lavender, now available in health food shops. Allow it to infuse for 15 minutes, then carefully strain into a small bowl with the honey. Mix, then add to the cooled custard; add the whipped cream, and transfer to the freezer. Stir occasionally to prevent large ice crystals forming. (An ice cream maker can also be used for this recipe.)

Serves 6

Primose and Violet Ice Bowl

Rarely will you come across a cheaper way of presenting a pudding, and in fact in my repertoire of favourite puds this is one of the most eye-catching serving bowls, which looks equally good for home-made sorbets. If the pudding course does not last for hours, or if you are a clever host, you can usually manage to slip the bowl away, rinse under the cold tap, and refreeze it.

To make the ice bowl you require two bowls, one almost half the size of the other. Fill the larger one with cold water, decorate with flowers around the edge, then place and anchor the smaller one inside with weights or ice cubes. Make sure the flowers remain in the correct place, then freeze for 10–14 hours. When it is removed from the freezer the small bowl should lift out easily, and the ice will slowly melt, allowing the ice bowl itself to lift out. Patience is needed here: plunging it into hot water is likely to spoil the finished result.

Rhubarb and Oaten Crumble

This is a most versatile pudding, which can be transformed to dinner-party status by the addition of a few muscatel raisins and the rind of one orange. The use of oats in the crumble gives this pudding a crunchy topping.

225 g (8 oz) sliced rhubarb
30 g (1 oz) caster or demerara sugar
A few slices of fresh angelica (to remove tartness)
55 g (2 oz) muscatel raisins
Rind of 1 orange

Topping

115 g (4 oz) coarse oatmeal
55 g (2 oz) fine oatmeal
55 g (2 oz) demerara sugar
55 g (2 oz) flaked almonds
55 g (2 oz) unsaturated fat

Slice the rhubarb and place it in a bowl with the sugar and angelica for a few hours before cooking; this helps to bring out the juices. Transfer to a serving dish and cover with the crumble, which is made by mixing the oatmeal, sugar and fat together until the mixture has the required texture. Pour on top of the fruit and bake at 190 °C (375 °F or regulo 5) for 15 minutes.

Serve sprinkled with toasted almonds, whipped cream, or a rich eggy custard.

Serves 6–8

Ring-a-Ring of Rosy Fruits

This beautifully simple yet sophisticated pudding has a wonderful, pure fruity flavour. Whole strawberries, blackberries, blackcurrants and blueberries are set in blackcurrant jelly in a ring mould with fresh fruit piled into the centre. If you are worried about unmoulding, make and serve the jellied pudding in glasses instead.

1 blackcurrant jelly
570 ml (1 pint) boiling water
Strawberries, blackcurrants, blackberries and blueberries to fill the mould

Italian Syrup

Rind and juice of 1 lemon and 1 orange
30 g (1 oz) caster sugar

Dissolve the jelly in 570 ml of boiling water; the quantity of the water may be reduced to 425 ml (¾ pint) to ensure a firm set, and this should make turning cut of the mould easier. Fill with fruit and pack the mould well. Cover the remainder of the fruit with orange and lemon juice and rind. Leave to sit for 1–2 hours to form a syrup. Unmould the jelly and fill the cavity with the fruit and syrup.

Serves 8–10

Fruitful Fool

Fruits such as strawberries, raspberries and apricots also make a good fruit fool. Strawberries and raspberries should be used without cooking.

450 g gooseberries
115 g sugar
2 tablesp. water
140 ml (¼ pint) cream

Top and tail the gooseberries. Wash and poach gently with the sugar and water until soft and pulped, then sieve. Whip the cream and combine with the fruit. Serve in small glasses and decorate with chocolate caraque, toasted pinhead oatmeal, and flaked almonds.

Serves 4

Summer Fruit Vacherin

A truly delightful pudding for that very special occasion, this is a layered meringue topped with an attractively piped trellis and sandwiched together with cream and an assortment of the scarlet summer fruits.

3 egg whites
170 g (6 oz) caster sugar
½ teasp. cornflour

Filling
280 ml (½ pint) lightly whipped cream
Assorted summer fruits

Make the meringue by beating the egg whites with half the caster sugar until very firm. Then carefully fold in the remaining sugar and cornflour. Transfer to a piping bag fitted with a rose pipe, and pipe out to give three circles, two in the form of a spiral and one trellised and finished around the edge with stars. Bake in a low oven at 120 °C (250 °F or regulo ½) for 45–60 minutes or until dry. When required, put together with the fruit and whipped cream.

This layered pudding will store unfilled in an airtight container for 1–2 weeks.

Serves 8

Fruit Compote

This is a very seasonal fresh fruit salad made with the scarlet summer fruits. The addition of the sugar-saver herb sweet cicely cuts down on the use of sugar by half in the making of the syrup.

Syrup
280 ml (½ pint) water
55 g (2 oz) caster sugar
5–6 leaves of sweet cicely

Compote
200 g (7 oz) approx. strawberries, raspberries, or loganberries
100 g (3½ oz) approx. redcurrants and blackcurrants
Juice of ½ lemon
1 apple } finely sliced into crescents
1 pear }

String the redcurrants and blackcurrants, and hull and slice the strawberries and raspberries, depending on their age. Pile these fruits into a bowl, sprinkling a little sugar between the layers if desired. A little lemon and orange juice can also be added to help form a delicate syrup. To make the syrup, boil the sugar and water for 1–2 minutes, add the sweet cicely, and leave to infuse for 5–10 minutes, then drain. As the syrup cools, add the sliced pear and apple.

Pour the fruits and syrup over the scarlet fruits, allow to cool slightly, and serve either warm or chilled with lightly whipped yoghurt trickled over the top.

Serves 8

Bramleys at their Best

Cooking apples must be among the most useful of all fruit, one of their great advantages being their low price in autumn; and they store so well throughout winter and well into the spring. Co. Armagh is renowned for its plentiful supply of Bramley apples. It is the use of apples and apricots, lightly spiced with cloves, cinnamon, and nutmeg, with a hint of lemony pastry, that makes this pudding so good. Just leave it to cook while you eat your main course.

3–4 cooking apples, peeled and sliced
115 g (4 oz) dried apricots
30 g (1 oz) sultanas, raisins, or prunes
A few cloves
½ teasp. cinnamon
A little freshly grated nutmeg
2–3 dessertsp. runny honey
Rind of ½ lemon
30 g (1 oz) demerara sugar

Pastry

85 g (3 oz) wholemeal flour
85 g (3 oz) self-raising flour
85 g (3 oz) butter
Rind and juice of 1 lemon, finely grated
A little milk to mix pastry

Make the pastry by mixing all the dry ingredients together. Cut and rub in the fat, and add the lemon rind and juice and the milk to mix to a firm dough. Alternatively, this pastry can equally well be made in a processor.

Prepare the fruits. Peel, core and slice the apples into wedges; the apricots may require steeping in cold water overnight. This pudding can be made in a variety of dishes: a 1.1 L (2 pint) pudding basin, an ovenproof dish or a baking tin. Roll out two-thirds of the pastry to line the base and sides of the basin. Fill with apples, apricots, sultanas, and demerara sugar, cover with spices, spoon over the honey, then seal the top with a pastry lid. Trim off the surplus pastry and bake at 190 °C (375 °F or regulo 5) for 25–30 minutes, or alternatively steam in a covered saucepan of boiling water for 1½ hours. (A very different result can be obtained with this pudding simply by the method of cooking.) Make sure the top of the pudding is covered with foil or greaseproof paper before steaming.

Serve hot with cream, yoghurt, or custard.

Serves 6–8

My Mum's King of Puddings

This was always the favourite Sunday pudding in our house. My mum varied the jams depending on the season, and this pudding tastes equally good with home-made rose-hip syrup.

570 ml (1 pint) milk
250 ml (½ pint) single cream
4 eggs
55 g (2 oz) sugar
30 g (1 oz) butter
Rind and juice of 1 lemon
225 g (8 oz) fresh white breadcrumbs
Jam to cover the bottom of the dish: rose-hip, wild strawberry, quince jelly, or damson

Put the milk and butter into a saucepan and heat gently. Pour over the breadcrumbs. Beat the cream lightly; in a separate bowl whisk the eggs, then mix together the breadcrumbs, eggs, milk, and melted butter, and finally the lightly whipped cream and the lemon rind and juice. Pour the breadcrumbs-and-custard mixture over the top of the jam, and bake in a moderate oven at 180 °C (350 °F or regulo 4) for 20–30 minutes.

Alternatively, use only the egg yolks for the base of this recipe, then the egg whites can be whisked with caster sugar to make a meringue for the top—55 g (2 oz) sugar to each egg white.

Serves 6

Topsy Orange and Turvy Ginger

This is a moist and spongy pudding for winter days, but livened up with oranges, and similar in many ways to the American upside-down cake, which is fun to make and looks most attractive. These cakes are usually served while still warm and with cream.

55 g (2 oz) butter
3 tablesp. brown sugar
2 small oranges

Gingerbread Sponge

115 g (4 oz) margarine or butter
115 g (4 oz) soft brown sugar
2 eggs, lightly whisked
170 g (6 oz) self-raising flour
1 teasp. baking powder
½ teasp. cloves
½ teasp. ginger powder
1 dessertsp. syrup
1 dessertsp. treacle
Rind and juice of ½ orange
A little milk to mix to a soft consistency

Melt the butter in the bottom of a 200 mm (7½–8½ in.) sandwich tin. Finely slice the oranges and arrange them around the bottom of the tin. Sprinkle with brown or demerara sugar. Cream the butter and sugar in a bowl until light and fluffy. Beat in the eggs gradually, alternately mixing with the flour, cloves, and ground ginger. Add the syrup, treacle, orange juice, and rind, mixing to a soft, dropping consistency. Spoon over the oranges, and bake in the centre of the oven, preheated to 180 °C (350 °F or regulo 4) for 1 hour.

If you like a darker gingerbread sponge, try this recipe, made by a slightly different method:

170 g (6 oz) flour
½ teasp. baking soda
½ teasp. ground ginger
Pinch of salt
30 g (1 oz) soft brown sugar
55 g (2 oz) butter or margarine
140 ml (¼ pint) lightly soured milk or buttermilk
1 dessertsp. syrup
1 dessertsp. treacle
1 egg

Sieve the flour, baking soda, salt and ginger into a bowl, add the sugar, and cut and rub in the fat. Pour the buttermilk into a pan, add the syrup and treacle, and warm them together. Use the beaten egg and buttermilk mixture to add to the flour, mixing to a heavy consistency. Spread over the oranges and bake without disturbing for 35–40 minutes at 180 °C (350 °F or regulo 4).

Serves 8–10